Crimes Against the Person

Scottish Criminal Law and Practice Series

Series Editor

The Rt Hon The Lord McCluskey

Crimes Against the Person

P W Ferguson LLB (Edin), Advocate

Edinburgh
Butterworths
1990

United Kingdom	Butterworth & Co (Publishers) Ltd, 88 Kingsway, LONDON WC2B 6AB and 4 Hill Street, EDINBURGH EH2 3JZ
Australia	Butterworths Pty Ltd, SYDNEY, MELBOURNE, BRISBANE, ADELAIDE, PERTH, CANBERRA and HOBART
Canada	Butterworths Canada Ltd, TORONTO and VANCOUVER
Ireland	Butterworth (Ireland) Ltd, DUBLIN
Malaysia	Malayan Law Journal Sdn Bhd, KUALA LUMPUR
New Zealand	Butterworths of New Zealand Ltd, WELLINGTON and AUCKLAND
Puerto Rico	Equity de Puerto Rico, Inc, HATO REY
Singapore	Butterworth & Co (Asia) Pte Ltd, SINGAPORE
USA	Butterworth Legal Publishers, ST PAUL, Minnesota, SEATTLE, Washington, BOSTON, Massachusetts, AUSTIN, Texas and D & S Publishers, CLEARWATER, Florida

All rights reserved. No part of this publication may be reproduced in any material form (including photocopying or storing it in any medium by electronic means and whether or not transiently or incidentally to some other use of this publication) without the written permission of the copyright owner except in accordance with the provisions of the Copyright, Designs and Patents Act 1988 or under the terms of a licence issued by the Copyright Licensing Agency Ltd, 33–34 Alfred Place, London, WC1E 7DP. Applications for the copyright owner's written permission to reproduce any part of this publication should be addressed to the publisher.

Warning: The doing of an unauthorised act in relation to a copyright work may result in both a civil claim for damages and criminal prosecution.

© Butterworth & Co (Publishers) Ltd 1990

A CIP Catalogue record for this book is available from the British Library

ISBN 0 406 14630 6

Typeset, printed and bound by Thomson Litho Ltd, East Kilbride, Scotland

Preface

This book is not intended as an academic study of the criminal law of Scotland. Indeed, the existence of Sheriff Gerald Gordon's excellent work, *The Criminal Law of Scotland*, would render pointless that objective. Rather this book is designed to serve as a statement of the criminal law regarding crimes against the person as it is understood and applied by the High Court of Justiciary.

The continuing and alarmingly large annual increase in criminal business which the High Court has to dispose of in the course of its sittings both as a court of first instance and as the appeal court, has given rise over the past decade to a considerable body of case law in the area of crimes against the person. This change is of course unsurprising since crimes such as assault, robbery, rape, culpable homicide and murder constitute a large proportion of the business of the criminal courts. It is therefore only appropriate that such an undoubtedly important part of the criminal law, which has been a hitherto much neglected area, should be recorded. This book is accordingly offered in the hope that it will be of some assistance to both practitioners and undergraduates who are concerned with, or in any event, interested in the criminal law of Scotland as it is interpreted, and developed, by Scotland's Supreme Court in matters criminal.

The law is stated as at 31 July 1990.

Finally, I should like to record my thanks to the staff of Butterworths in Edinburgh for their assistance with the preparation of this book.

P W Ferguson
Parliament House
Edinburgh

August 1990

Contents

Preface v
Abbreviations ix
Table of statutes xi
Table of cases xiii

1. Assault 1
2. Murder 12
3. Culpable homicide 22
4. Rape 28
5. Robbery 34
6. Incest and related offences 40
7. Physical offences involving indecency 44
8. Self defence 47
9. Provocation 56
10. Diminished responsibility 62
11. Joint responsibility for crimes against the person 68
12. Miscellaneous general defences 74

Index 85

Abbreviations

Case Reports

AC	Law Reports, Appeal Cases (House of Lords and Privy Council) 1890–
Adam	Adam's Justiciary Reports 1894–1919
All ER	All England Law Reports 1936–
Arkley	Arkley's Justiciary Reports 1846–48
Cl & Fin	Clark and Finnelly's Reports (House of Lords) 1831–46
Coup	Couper's Justiciary Reports 1868–85
Cr App Rep	Criminal Appeal Reports (England) 1908–
Crim LR	Criminal Law Review (England) 1954–
GWD	Green's Weekly Digest 1986–
HKLR	Hong Kong Law Reports
Irv	Irvine's Justiciary Reports 1851–68
JC	Justiciary Cases 1917–
JCL	Journal of Criminal Law
JR	Juridical Review 1889–
P	Law Reports, Probate, Divorce and Admiralty Division (England) 1890–1971
QB	Queen's Bench Reports (England) 1841–52 (volume number precedes)
QB	Law Reports, Queen's Bench Division (England) 1891–1901, 1952– (year precedes)
RTR	Road Traffic Reports 1970–
SCCR	Scottish Criminal Case Reports 1981–
SCCR Supp	Scottish Criminal Case Reports Supplement 1950–80
SLT	Scots Law Times 1893–1908 (preceded by year and volume number), and 1909– (preceded by year)
Swin	Swinton's Justiciary Reports 1835–41

Syme   Syme's Justiciary Reports 1826–29
VLR   Victorian Law Reports 1875–1956
White   White's Justiciary Reports 1885–93

Textbooks

Alison *Principles:* Archibald Alison *Principles of the Criminal Law of Scotland* (1832)

Gordon: G H Gordon *The Criminal Law of Scotland* (2nd edn, 1978) (Supplement 1984)

Hume: David Hume *Commentaries on the Law of Scotland, Respecting the Description and Punishment of Crimes* (2 vols, 1797) (reprinted 1986)

Macdonald: J H A Macdonald *The Criminal Law of Scotland* (5th edn, 1948, by J Walker and D J Stevenson) (reprinted 1986)

Renton and Brown: R W Renton and H H Brown *Criminal Procedure according to the Law of Scotland* (5th edn, 1983, by G H Gordon)

Table of statutes

	PARA
Aviation Security Act 1982	5.13
Criminal Justice (Scotland) Act 1980	7.03
s 80(7)(c)	7.04
(11)	7.04, 7.08
Criminal Law Amendment Act 1885	
s 4	4.09
5(2)	4.12
Criminal Procedure (Scotland) Act 1975	
s 46	11.03
174(2), (3)	12.09
175	10.05, 10.08, 10.09
(4)	10.05
205(1)	10.08
312(d)	11.03
Family Law (Scotland) Act 1985	
s 1(1)(d)	6.05
Hijacking Act 1971	5.13
Incest Act 1567	6.01, 6.08
Incest and Related Offences (Scotland) Act 1986	6.01, 6.02, 6.03
s 2A(2)	6.03
Mental Health (Scotland) Act 1960	12.19
Mental Health (Scotland) Act 1984	10.09
s 17(1)(a)(i)	10.08
(ii)	10.09

	PARA
Police (Scotland) Act 1967	
s 41(1)(a)	1.12
Road Traffic Act 1972	3.10
s 1	3.12
2	1.31
6(1)	12.03, 12.04
Road Traffic Act 1988	
s 1	2.01, 3.10, 3.11, 3.12
Sexual Offences (Scotland) Act 1976	6.02, 6.04
s 2(2)	4.09
2A	6.03, 6.08
2B	6.05, 6.06, 6.08
2C	6.07, 6.08
3	7.07
(1), (2)	4.11
4(1)	7.07, 7.08
(2)(a), (b)	7.08
5	7.06
13	4.11
Tokyo Convention Act 1967	5.11, 5.12, 5.13
s 1(1)–(3)	5.13
4	5.12
Sch, art 15	5.12
Treason Act 1842	
s 2	1.11

Table of cases

PARA
Advocate (HM) v Blake 1986 SLT 661 ..... 3.13, 10.01, 10.04, 10.06, 10.07, 12.10
Advocate (HM) v Braithwaite 1945 JC 55 .... 10.02
Advocate (HM) v Brogan 1964 SLT 204 .... 8.03
Advocate (HM) v Brown (1879) 4 Coup 225 .... 2.08
Advocate (HM) v Callander 1958 SLT 24 .... 9.06
Advocate (HM) v Campbell 1921 JC 1 .... 12.15
Advocate (HM) v Carson 1964 SLT 21 .... 1.22, 8.02, 8.03, 9.10
Advocate (HM) v Charles Sweenie (1858) 3 Irv 109 .... 4.08, 4.10
Advocate (HM) v Cunningham 1963 JC 80, 1963 SLT 345 .... 10.01, 12.18, 12.19
Advocate (HM) v D 1952 SCCR 182 .... 4.01
Advocate (HM) v Delaney 1946 SLT 25 .... 3.04
Advocate (HM) v Doherty 1954 JC 1 .... 8.07, 8.08, 8.10, 8.11
Advocate (HM) v Fagen (1838) 2 Swin 25 .... 5.04
Advocate (HM) v Fraser (1847) Arkley 280 .... 4.09
Advocate (HM) v Fraser and Rollins 1923 JC 60 .... 2.14
Advocate (HM) v Grainger and Rae 1932 JC 40 .... 4.01, 4.12
Advocate (HM) v Greig (May 1979, unreported) 9.08
Advocate (HM) v Hartley 1989 SLT 135 .... 2.16, 2.17, 3.01, 3.05
Advocate (HM) v Hawton & Parker (1861) 4 Irv 58 .... 2.05
Advocate (HM) v Hayes (November 1949, unreported) 12.18
Advocate (HM) v Hill 1941 JC 59 .... 9.06, 9.07
Advocate (HM) v Kidd 1960 JC 61, 1960 SLT 82 ...... 12.10, 12.11, 12.13, 12.20
Advocate (HM) v Kizilevieczius 1938 JC 60, 1938 SLT 245 ... 8.04, 8.05, 9.02, 9.03
Advocate (HM) v Lappen 1956 SLT 109 .... 11.01
Advocate (HM) v Logan 1935 JC 100 .... 4.10
Advocate (HM) v McCallum (19 May 1977, unreported) 12.07
Advocate (HM) v McDonald and Dunstan (1872) 2 Coup 174 .... 1.10
Advocate (HM) v McGinlay 1983 SLT 562 .... 2.07
Advocate (HM) v McGuiness 1937 JC 37 .... 2.18
Advocate (HM) v McManimy & Higgins (1847) Arkley 321 .... 2.06
Advocate (HM) v McPhee 1935 JC 46 .... 2.06
Advocate (HM) v Miller and Denovan (November 1960, unreported) 2.20
Advocate (HM) v Montgomery 1926 JC 2 .... 4.09
Advocate (HM) v Myles Martin (1886) 1 White 297 .... 1.14
Advocate (HM) v Paxton 1985 SLT 96 .... 4.01
Advocate (HM) v Peters (1969) 33 JCL 209 .... 12.08
Advocate (HM) v Phipps (1905) 4 Adam 616 .... 1.03, 1.30, 1.32
Advocate (HM) v Raiker 1989 SCCR 149 .... 12.16
Advocate (HM) v Ritchie 1926 JC 45 .... 12.18
Advocate (HM) v Robertson & Donoghue (August 1975, unreported) 2.10
Advocate (HM) v Rutherford 1947 JC 1 .... 1.16, 8.17

xiii

xiv TABLE OF CASES

	PARA
Advocate (HM) v Savage 1923 JC 49, 1923 SLT 659	10.02
Advocate (HM) v Sheppard 1941 JC 69	2.05
Advocate (HM) v Slaven (1885) 5 Coup 694	2.12
Advocate (HM) v Smith (February 1952, unreported)	9.09
Advocate (HM) v Thom (1876) 3 Coup 332	1.04
Advocate (HM) v Welsh and McLachlan (1897) 5 SLT 137	11.12
Advocate (HM) v Williamson (1866) 5 Irv 326	2.13
Advocate (HM) v Woods 1972 SLT (Notes) 77	8.18, 11.04
Allan v HM Advocate 1983 SCCR 183	10.05, 10.08
Allan v Patterson 1980 SLT 77	1.31, 3.10, 3.11, 3.12
Atkinson v HM Advocate 1987 SCCR 534	1.01
Attorney-General's reference (No 6 of 1980) [1981] QB 715	1.17
B v Harris 1990 SLT 208	1.28
Barbour v HM Advocate 1982 SCCR 195	4.07
Beckford v R [1987] 3 All ER 425	8.09, 8.16
Berry v HM Advocate 1976 SCCR Supp 156	9.04
Bird v HM Advocate 1952 JC 23	2.08, 3.05
Bonar v McLeod 1983 SCCR 161	1.23, 2.06
Brady v HM Advocate 1986 SCCR 191, 1986 SLT 686	3.13, 9.02, 9.12, 10.07
Brennan v HM Advocate 1977 SLT 151	10.01, 12.11, 12.13, 12.15, 12.16, 12.20
Brown v Hilson 1924 JC 1	1.13
C v HM Advocate 1987 SCCR 104	1.03, 1.17
CR v Tyrrell [1894] 1 QB 710	7.07
Cameron v HM Advocate 1971 JC 50	5.10, 5.11
Capuano v HM Advocate 1984 SCCR 415	11.04
Carmichael v Boyle 1985 SCCR 58	12.19, 12.20
Carraher v HM Advocate 1946 JC 108	10.02, 10.03, 10.04, 10.05
Cawthorne v HM Advocate 1968 JC 32	2.14, 4.06, 9.12
Codona v Cardle 1989 SLT 791	1.26
Connelly v HM Advocate (5 June 1990, unreported)	10.02, 10.04
Connor v Jessop 1988 SCCR 624	1.03
Connorton v Annan 1981 SCCR 307	12.05
Cosgrove v HM Advocate (28 March 1990, unreported)	9.04
Jas Craw (1826) Syme 188	8.14
Crawford v HM Advocate 1950 JC 67, 1950 SLT 279	8.03, 8.05, 8.15, 8.17, 9.02, 9.08
Cromar v HM Advocate 1987 SCCR 635	5.04
Dickie v HM Advocate (1897) 2 Adam 331	4.01
Donaldson v HM Advocate 1983 SCCR 216	10.08
Dunn v HM Advocate 1960 JC 55	3.11
Elliott v HM Advocate 1987 SCCR 278	8.13
Farrell v Stevenson 1975 SLT (Sh Ct) 71	12.19
Fenning v HM Advocate 1985 SCCR 219, 1985 SLT 540	1.21, 8.05, 8.06, 8.11, 9.02
Finlayson v HM Advocate 1978 SLT (Notes) 60	2.02, 2.11, 2.13
Fraser v Skinner 1975 SLT (Notes) 84	1.21
Simon Fraser (1878) 4 Coup 70	12.18
Fulton (Robert), Junior (1841) 2 Swin 564	4.03

TABLE OF CASES xv

	PARA
Gilmour v HM Advocate 1938 SLT 72	3.04
Gizzi v Tudhope 1982 SCCR 442, 1983 SLT 214	1.31, 1.32, 3.11
Graham v Annan 1980 SLT 28	12.05
Graham v HM Advocate 1987 SCCR 20	8.17, 9.08
Grant v Allan 1988 SLT 11	5.02
Gray v Hawthorn 1964 JC 69	1.27, 1.28
Guest v Annan 1988 SCCR 275	1.28
Hancock v HM Advocate 1981 JC 74	11.07
Hendry v HM Advocate 1988 SLT 25	2.07, 2.09
Hillan v HM Advocate 1937 JC 53, 1937 SLT 396	8.04, 8.05, 8.11, 9.02
Jones v HM Advocate 1989 SCCR 726	8.09, 8.15, 9.11
Kay v Allan (1978) SCCR Supp 188	1.01
Kennedy (1829)	8.14
Kennedy v HM Advocate 1944 JC 171	12.15
Kennedy v HM Advocate 1950 JC 67	8.17
Kennedy v Young (1854) 1 Irv 533	1.29
Kerr v HM Advocate 1986 SCCR 91	1.04
Khaliq v HM Advocate 1984 SLT 137	1.32, 2.11
Kwok Chak Ming (No 1) v The Queen [1963] HKLR 226	2.01
Lambie v HM Advocate 1973 SLT 219	12.14
Lourie v HM Advocate 1988 SCCR 634	2.09, 3.06
Lynch v DPP for Northern Ireland [1975] AC 653	12.08
McCluskey v HM Advocate 1959 JC 39, 1959 SLT 215	3.04, 8.08, 8.13, 8.15
McCluskey v HM Advocate 1988 SCCR 629	2.01, 3.10
McDermott v HM Advocate 1976 JC 8	9.06
McDermott v HM Advocate 1974 SLT 206	3.04
McGhie (1971)	9.10
McGregor v HM Advocate (1973) SCCR Supp 54	12.16
Mackenzie v HM Advocate 1983 SLT 220	8.17, 8.18
MacLeod v MacDougall 1988 SCCR 519	12.04, 12.05
McNab v Guild 1989 SCCR 138	12.04, 12.05
McNaghten's Case (1843) 10 Cl & Fin 200	12.11
MacNeill v Robertson 1982 SCCR 468	11.08
MacPhail v Clark 1983 SCCR 395	2.06
Mack v HM Advocate 1959 SLT 288	4.12
Malone v HM Advocate 1988 SCCR 498	2.20, 3.07, 11.02
Marchbank v Annan 1987 SCCR 718	1.23
Mathieson v HM Advocate 1981 SCCR 196	3.06
Meek v HM Advocate 1982 SCCR 613, 1983 SLT 280	4.04, 8.16
Melvin v HM Advocate 1984 SCCR 113, 1984 SLT 365	2.20, 3.07, 11.02
Miller v HM Advocate 1987 GWD 7–216	10.07
Milne v Tudhope 1981 SLT (Notes) 42	5.02
Moore v MacDougall 1989 SCCR 659	8.11
Mowles v HM Advocate 1986 SCCR 117	3.06
O'Connell v HM Advocate 1987 SCCR 459	11.01, 11.13
O'Neill v HM Advocate 1934 JC 98	5.04
Oropesa, The [1943] P 32	2.11

	PARA
Owens v HM Advocate 1946 JC 119	8.08, 8.15, 9.11
Paton v HM Advocate 1935 JC 19	3.08, 3.09
People v Lewis 124 Cal 551, 57 Pac (1899)	2.07, 2.12
Re Piracy jure gentium [1934] AC 586	5.09
Quinn v Cunningham 1956 JC 22	1.31
Quinn v HM Advocate 1990 SCCR 254	4.05
R v Bird [1985] 2 All ER 513	8.10
R v Blaue [1975] 3 All ER 446	2.12
R v Conway [1989] RTR 35	12.04
R v Gibbins and Proctor (1918) 13 Cr App Rep 134	2.06
R v HM Advocate 1988 SCCR 254, 1988 SLT 623	6.09
R v Howe [1987] 1 All ER 771	12.08
R v Morgan [1976] AC 182	4.04
R v Russell [1933] VLR 59	2.06
R v Williams [1987] 3 All ER 411	8.16
RHW v HM Advocate 1982 SCCR 152	1.31, 1.32
Roberts v Hamilton 1989 SLT 399	1.03, 1.30
S v HM Advocate 1989 SLT 469	1.19, 4.01
Sayers v HM Advocate 1981 SCCR 312	11.09, 11.11
Sinclair v HM Advocate (4 May 1990, unreported)	11.01
Smart v HM Advocate 1975 JC 30, 1975 SLT 65	1.03, 1.16
Socratous v HM Advocate 1987 SLT 244	11.06
Stallard v HM Advocate 1989 SCCR 248	11.03
Stewart v Thain 1981 SLT (Notes) 2	1.27
Stirling v Annan 1983 SCCR 396	12.19
Stobbs v HM Advocate 1983 SCCR 190	9.04
Surman v HM Advocate 1988 SLT 371	8.18
Sweeney v X 1982 SCCR 509	4.10
Taylor v HM Advocate (June 1975, unreported)	2.09
Thomas v HM Advocate (16 March, 15 June 1990 unreported)	10.08
Thomson v HM Advocate 1983 SLT 682	12.06, 12.07
Thomson v HM Advocate 1985 SCCR 448	9.04, 9.05, 9.07, 9.08, 9.09
Tudhope v Grubb 1983 SCCR 350	12.03, 12.04
Walker and Raiker v HM Advocate 1985 SCCR 150	11.12
Watt v Annan 1978 SLT 198 1978 JC 84	6.09
Winnik v Allan 1986 SCCR 35	11.08
Young v HM Advocate 1932 JC 63	11.04

1. Assault

Introduction

1.01 The crime of assault is constituted by any attack upon the person of another whether or not the attack results in injury[1]. An assault is constituted by threatening gestures sufficient to produce alarm, such as a masked man jumping over a shop counter and running towards a cashier[2]. However, mere words alone cannot constitute assault although the use of certain threats are themselves criminal albeit not the crime of assault[3]. Equally, an assault can be committed by setting dogs on the victim[4], irrespective of whether or not the victim is bitten[5]. Assault can also be committed on a sleeping person who need not apprehend any fear or sense any pain as the result of the assailant's actings; and can be committed indirectly by, for example, violently stopping a horse which the victim is riding, thereby throwing the victim to the ground[6].

1 J H A Macdonald *The Criminal Law of Scotland* (5th edn, 1948), p 115; G H Gordon *The Criminal Law of Scotland* (2nd edn, 1978) (Supp 1984), para 29–01.
2 *Atkinson v HM Advocate* 1987 SCCR 534.
3 See *James Millar* (1862) 4 Irv 238.
4 *Macdonald* p 115. *Kay v Allan* (1978) SCCR Supp 188.
5 *Macdonald* p 115.
6 *Macdonald* p 115; *Gordon* para 29–01.

1.02 Since any attempt at crime is itself a crime, it follows that Scots law recognises the crime of attempted assault. However, the distinction must necessarily be a theoretical one. Since any attack upon the person of another constitutes assault, and the attack need not be successful (for example A aims a blow at B but misses), there is no practical use in the courts employing the concept of attempted assault. All attempted assaults are therefore in practice referred to and described as assault.

Mens rea

1.03 Macdonald states that evil intention is of the essence of assault[1] and this view has been repeated on many occasions[2]. It has thus been accepted that assault cannot be committed recklessly or negligently[3]. It is, after all, strange to talk of an attack as being anything other than an intentional act. However, the High Court has authoritatively stated in *Roberts v Hamilton*[4] that where injury to any person is an event which is likely to occur, the assailant is answerable for it as an assault[5].

Thus where A and B are struggling with each other, and C, intending to strike A, misses A and instead unintentionally strikes B, C is guilty of assault and not simply of recklessly causing injury to B. However, it is necessary that there be an intention on the part of the assailant to cause injury to someone. If the assailant's act is not directed against the person of anyone, he will not be guilty of assault because he will lack the necessary *mens rea*[6]. Where, therefore, A discharges a shotgun at a bush and is unaware of the presence of B behind the bush, A is not guilty of assault although he will in certain circumstances be guilty of culpably and recklessly causing injury to B.

Accordingly the so-called doctrine of transferred intent (whereby an intention on the part of A to injure B is sufficient to criminalise the unintentional injury caused to C) applies in Scotland in relation to the crime of assault. It remains to be decided, however, whether A is guilty of two assaults where he intends to injure B but in the process injures both B and C. A never intended to injure C but was aware of the presence of C. On the *ratio* of *Connor v Jessop*[7] and *Roberts v Hamilton*, there is no reason in principle why A should not be guilty of assaulting both B and C.

1 *Macdonald* p 115.
2 See eg *Smart v HM Advocate* 1975 JC 30; *C v HM Advocate* 1987 SCCR 104.
3 *Gordon* para 29–30; see also *HM Advocate v Phipps* (1905) 4 Adam 616.
4 1989 SLT 399.
5 See also *Connor v Jessop* 1988 SCCR 624.
6 See *Roberts v Hamilton* 1989 SLT 399 at 401; *Macdonald* p 115.
7 1988 SCCR 624.

Aggravated assault

1.04 The charge of assault can be rendered more serious, or aggravated, by various additional allegations. The commonest allegations are that the assault is to the victim's severe injury, his permanent impairment or disfigurement, or the danger of his life. It is now unknown for the Crown to libel a charge of assault with intent to kill. In the case of assault to the danger of life, the Crown need not prove actual injury since the aggravating circumstance is the endangerment of the victim's life which can be inferred from the nature of the acts perpetrated by the assailant[1].

Moreover, in all of these cases of aggravations it is unnecessary for the Crown to lead evidence sufficient to establish that the accused actually intended to inflict the particular degree of injury sustained by the victim. These aggravations are to be objectively determined by the jury on the evidence.

1 *Kerr v HM Advocate* 1986 SCCR 91; *HM Advocate v Thom* (1876) 3 Coup 332.

1.05 It is correctly stated by Macdonald[1] that assault to the danger of life is almost always tried in the High Court but Sheriff Gordon[2] states misleadingly that cases of assault to severe injury are often dealt with by the High Court. The vast majority of such charges are now prosecuted on indictment in the sheriff court and where necessary, are remitted to the High Court for sentence.

1 *Macdonald* p 118.
2 *Gordon* para 29–06.

1.06 Macdonald[1] notes that assault may also be aggravated by (1) the mode of perpetration of the assault; (2) the place where the assault is committed; or (3) the character of the person who is assaulted.

1 *Macdonald* p 117; see also *Gordon* paras 29–04 to 29–20.

The mode of perpetration

1.07 The commonest aggravation of assault arising out of the mode of perpetrating assault is the use of a weapon whether it be a club, knife, razor, broken bottle or other instrument. It is unnecessary for actual injury to have been inflicted upon the victim. The most important of these aggravations are assaults by stabbing or cutting with a knife or similar instrument; the use of a firearm whether or not it is loaded, or the use of an imitation incapable of being discharged; and the throwing of acid or other corrosive or burning substance. Under the last category it is, for example, a serious aggravation to pour petrol on a victim and threaten to ignite the petrol.

The place of the crime

1.08 In former times there was a particular variety of aggravated assault referred to by the *nomen iuris* of hamesucken. Hamesucken was an assault committed upon a man in his own house, the house having been entered for that purpose[1]. As such it was a capital crime at common law until 1887. It is however still an example of an aggravation of assault although the *nomen iuris* has fallen into desuetude.

1 *Hume* I, 327; Alison Principles p 199; *Macdonald* p 118.

1.09 It is also an aggravation to commit assault within the precincts of the High Court of Justiciary or the Court of Session[1]. It does not, however, appear to be an aggravation of the crime to commit assault in the sheriff court or district court[2]. It was, and undoubtedly still is (at least theoretically), an aggravation of the crime to commit assault 'in the presence of the Sovereign or in the Royal domain'[3].

1 *Hume* I, 405; *Macdonald* p 118; *Gordon* para 29–08.
2 If assault is committed within any courtroom, and in the presence of the presiding judge, it is also undoubtedly a contempt of court.
3 *Macdonald* p 118; *Hume* I, 326–327.

The character of the victim

1.10 Assaults committed upon particular victims can be aggravated by the character of the victims. For example, it is an aggravation of assault to attack a child, or a very old person, probably because both are defenceless. It is also an aggravation that the victim is a Senator of the College of Justice, or a sheriff or justice of the peace engaged in judicial duties. It is apparently not, however, an aggravation to assault a member of the Faculty of Advocates as he is about to enter court[1].

1 *HM Advocate v McDonald and Dunstan* (1872) 2 Coup 174; *Gordon* para 29–14 (note 57).

1.11 It is a very serious aggravation of the crime to assault the Sovereign, and such an offence may amount to high treason or treason felony[1]. Assault upon the person of the Sovereign is also an offence under the Treason Act 1842, s 2 and punishable by a maximum of seven years' imprisonment.

1 *Gordon* para 29–16.

Assaults on officers of law

1.12 It is an aggravation of assault that it is committed upon an officer of the law engaged in the execution of his duty[1]. The category of such officers is not restricted to police officers (for whom there is in any event, a separate offence under the Police (Scotland) Act 1967, s 41(1)(a)), but extends to messengers-at-arms, sheriff officers, officers of the Inland Revenue, justices of the peace engaged in suppressing a riot, and persons known to be assisting such officers in the discharge of their duties[2].

1 *Macdonald* p 118.

2 *Gordon* para 29–11. Scots law recognises the separate crime of deforcement which consists of forcibly preventing officers of the law from executing a judicial warrant but such a use of force is now treated as a mere aggravation of assault (*Macdonald* p 168).

Breach of trust

1.13 A further accepted aggravating feature of the crime of assault is any assault involving a breach of trust. For example, assaults by parents and guardians on their children, and by schoolteachers on their pupils[1] are aggravated crimes. Equally, a police officer who assaults his prisoner, or a prison officer who asaults a prison inmate, abuses his position of authority, and thereby aggravates the assault which he commits.

1 Eg *Brown v Hilson* 1924 JC 1.

Knowledge of the nature of the character of the victim

1.14 It has already been noted that aggravations constituted by the degree of injury do not require to be intended[1]. However, it is essential that the Crown prove that the accused knew of the nature of the character of his victim. There is no difficulty with children and old people, nor with judges or the Sovereign, but difficulty arises in respect of officers of law who are not in uniform or otherwise easily identifiable. There requires to be some form of evidence from which it can be inferred that the accused either knew or ought reasonably to have known that the victim was a plain clothes police officer, messenger-at-arms, or other officer of the law[2].

1 See para 1.07, above.
2 *HM Advocate v Myles Martin* (1886) 1 White 297; *Gordon* para 29–21.

Intention to commit an ulterior or further crime

1.15 Finally, the assault can be aggravated by being committed with intent to commit an ulterior or further crime. For example, assault with intent to rob, or to rape (formerly ravish) or pervert the course of justice, are aggravated assaults. Most but not all assaults committed with intent to commit a further crime are themselves attempts at the further crime.

Consent as a defence

1.16 In *Smart v HM Advocate*[1] the High Court held that since consent is not a defence in cases of murder or culpable homicide[2] or assault to the danger of life, there is no justification for its being a defence to minor assaults. Lord Justice-Clerk Wheatley explained:

'Apart from the obvious difficulty of knowing where to draw the line there is nothing in principle to justify the distinction. If there is an attack on the other person and it is done with evil intent, that is, intent to injure and do bodily harm, then, in our view, the fact that the person attacked was willing to undergo the risk of that attack does not prevent it from being the crime of assault.'

1 1975 SLT 65.
2 *Hume* I, 230; *HM Advocate v Rutherford* 1947 JC 1.

1.17 It is clear therefore that evil intent is the distinguishing feature between criminal and non-criminal physical contact between persons. Thus in *Smart* the court explained that if A touches B in a sexual manner with B's consent (and there is nothing else involved which would constitute a crime under statute or at common law[1]) there is no assault. Nor is there assault when persons engage in sporting activities governed by rules which permit some form of violence because, as the Lord Justice-Clerk said in *Smart*, '[t]he intention is to engage in the sporting activity and not evilly to do harm to the opponent'. This distinction is clearly difficult to support in the case of professional boxers. Thus it is clear that the decision in *Smart* was, at the end of the day, a public policy decision. The court indeed even remarked on the public policy implications of its decision. As Lord Lane CJ said in a similar case in England[2]: 'It is not in the public interest that people should try to cause, or should cause, each other actual bodily harm for no good reason'[3].

1 Cf indecent assault involving girls under twelve years of age: *C v HM Advocate* 1987 SCCR 104.
2 *Attorney-General's reference (No 6 of 1980)* [1981] QB 715 at 719.
3 The Court of Appeal in England has held that the intentional infliction of any degree of bodily harm however slight, is a crime unless the victim consents and the action can be justified as being not against the public interest: Smith and Hogan *Criminal Law* (6th edn, 1988) p 386.

1.18 Sheriff Gordon states that where there is no intention to do bodily harm, consent may still be a defence to assault because the court in *Smart* accepted that touching a consenting partner in a sexual manner was not assault as the necessary intent was absent in such a case[1]. However, the truth of this proposition depends on the meaning ascribed to the word 'harm' used by the court in *Smart*. An intention evilly to do harm does not necessarily mean *only* an intention to do bodily harm. It is accordingly submitted here that consent is not a defence to any type of assault.

1 *Gordon* para 29–39.

1.19 It should be noted, however, that while *Smart* makes consent irrelevant in cases of assault, it is not the law that consent is irrelevant in cases of rape. Despite the fact that the High Court in *S v HM Advocate*[1] described rape as being no more than an aggravated assault, rape is not merely an aggravation of assault. The Crown requires to prove absence of consent to sexual intercourse in a charge of rape[2] and accordingly, consent is a defence to a charge of rape.

1 1989 SLT 469 at 473.
2 See ch 4, below.

The lawful use of force

1.20 The two principal circumstances in which a person is entitled to use force against another person without committing an assault are cases involving private defence and cases of reasonable force being used to prevent crime. Other categories of the justified use of force are the right of a parent, guardian or schoolteacher to punish his child or pupil, and the right of a landowner or an occupier of land to eject a trespasser upon his land.

Private defence

1.21 This category of the justified use of force is in truth a particular subdivision of the use of force in the prevention of crime. If A is attacked by B with his fists and feet, A is entitled to defend himself if he has no reasonable opportunity of retreating or avoiding conflict with B. A's plea of self-defence in a charge of assault will, however, be defeated if his use of force amounts to cruel excess[1]. Thus, A is not entitled to retaliate with a crowbar, or continue to strike B after B is disabled. Similarly, if A is attacked by B carrying a knife, once B is disarmed, A cannot thereafter continue to punch and kick B. The test is always whether A's conduct is cruelly excessive and in applying that test, the evidence should not be weighed in too fine scales and allowance should be made as, Lord Cameron expressed it, for 'the excitement or state of fear or heat of blood at the moment of attack'[2]. Self-defence is also available to an accused person if he used appropriate force to ward off what he reasonably apprehended was an imminent attack upon his person[3].

1 *Fraser v Skinner* 1975 SLT (Notes) 84; *Macdonald* p 116.
2 *Fenning v HM Advocate* 1985 SCCR 219 at 225, 1985 SLT 540 at 543.
3 For self-defence, see ch 8, below.

1.22 In *HM Advocate v Carson*[1] one of two men who were charged with aggravated assault, pled self-defence on the basis that he acted in order to stop a homicidal attack by the victim on his co-accused. Lord Wheatley (as he then was) directed the jury:

'If a man sees another man being unlawfully attacked he is entitled to try to stop that unlawful attack, and if within reason he uses methods that otherwise would constitute an assault he will be excused because his intention is not to commit a criminal assault on the victim but to prevent the victim from carrying out an assault, an illegitimate assault, on another person'.

Thus, the principles of self-defence apply equally in the case where the attack, or the reasonably apprehended attack, is upon another person.

1 1964 SLT 21.

The prevention of crime

1.23 A police officer is entitled to use reasonable force in preventing a crime and in arresting or detaining a person. He must not, however, use excessive force; the force must be reasonable in the circumstances. Thus, where a police officer, after a motor car chase, broke open the car window, struck the 16-year-old driver on the head with his truncheon, pulled him from the car and kicked him while he crouched on the ground, the High Court upheld the conviction for assault on the view that what the police officer did 'went far beyond the limit of the force which a police officer is entitled to apply when attempting to apprehend a suspect'[1].

1 *Marchbank v Annan* 1987 SCCR 718 at 721. See also *Bonar v McLeod* 1983 SCCR 161.

1.24 Equally, a private person is entitled to assist a police officer engaged in preventing crime or arresting or detaining a person. If, for example, A saw a police officer attempting to apprehend a thief who was attempting to run off, A would be entitled to use reasonable force to detain the thief. The test in such circumstances, unlike cases of private defence, is whether the force used is reasonable. It is not only the high test of cruel excess which elides the defence; unreasonable force will also suffice to lose the accused his entitlement to use force at all.

1.25 A private person also has a right at common law to use reasonable force to detain any one who is committing a serious crime[1]. The power to effect a 'citizen's arrest' is similar to a police officer's right to arrest without warrant, but the crime in question must be serious if a private citizen is to be permitted to use reasonable force.

1 *Gordon* para 29–35; Renton and Brown *Criminal Procedure according to the Law of Scotland* (5th edn, 1983) para 5–19.

1.26 The test in such circumstances is also whether reasonable force is used. In *Codona v Cardle*[1] A, a proprietor of an amusement arcade who believed that B had deliberately broken a window in the arcade, was held to have used excessive force in grabbing B by the arm and twisting his arm behind his back when B refused A's request to go with him to the local police station[1].

1 1989 SLT 791, High Court of Justiciary. In this case the High Court did not accept that on the findings-in-fact A was entitled to effect a 'citizen's arrest'.

The right to punish children

1.27 It is the right of parents, guardians, schoolteachers and other persons having charge of children, to employ reasonable force for the purpose of disciplining them[1]. Schoolteachers possess this power of chastisement in order to enable them to do their educational work and to maintain proper order in class and in school[2]. Since they exercise the power by virtue of their office as a teacher and not as an agent of the child's parents, the right is properly exercisable only within school. However, a schoolteacher (and presumably any other person) can be authorised by a parent to exercise the right to chastise *in loco parentis*[3].

1 *Gordon* para 29–38.
2 *Gray v Hawthorn* 1964 JC 69.
3 Eg *Stewart v Thain* 1981 SLT (Notes) 2.

1.28 Schoolteachers, parents and others can, however, be convicted of assault committed upon their children if an evil intent can be proved against them, as was stated by Lord Guthrie in *Gray v Hawthorn*[1] where it was pointed out that the existence of evil intent in the mind of an accused person must always be a question to be decided in the light of the whole circumstances. If, for example, malice or persecution can be made out, then a conviction for assault can be obtained. It is not, however, sufficient for the purposes of evil intent that the parent or schoolteacher was angry when he administered punishment[2]. Evil intent can also be established by evidence of excessive force[3].

1 1964 JC 69.
2 *Guest v Annan* 1988 SCCR 275; *B v Harris* 1990 SLT 208.
3 See *B v Harris* above.

Assault in defence of property

1.29 Sheriff Gordon notes that there is little authority regarding assaults committed in defence of proprietory rights[1]. As a matter of principle it seems unacceptable in modern times that violence can be committed merely to prevent damage to property unless the threatened damage is very serious[2]. For example, A pours petrol through a letterbox of an unoccupied house owned by B, with the intention of igniting the petrol. B assaults A with a stick causing moderate injury forcing A to run off, and thereby B saves his property from destruction. A poses no threat to life or limb, only to property; B does not purport to exercise a 'citizen's right' to arrest A. There is, however, no modern judicial decision supporting B's right to commit assault in these circumstances.

1 *Gordon* para 29–35.
2 Cf *Kennedy v Young* (1854) 1 Irv 533.

Culpable and reckless conduct

1.30 Until the decision in *Roberts v Hamilton*[1] the traditional view was that assault required an intentional attack, but that if an evil intent could not be proved, the infliction of injury could still be criminal if the harm was inflicted as a result of culpable and reckless conduct. Thus it was not uncommon for the Crown to libel assault and alternatively, the culpable and reckless causing of injury[2]. Such a precaution is not now necessary in the light of the decision in *Roberts v Hamilton*[3].

1 1989 SLT 399.
2 See eg *HM Advocate v Phipps* (1905) 4 Adam 616.
3 See paras 1.03–1.05, above.

1.31 Not all unintentional injury is criminal and thus not all culpable and reckless conduct is punishable. It is of the essence of culpable and reckless conduct that there should be criminal recklessness in the sense of 'a total indifference to and disregard for the safety of the public'. This test was provided in *R H W v HM Advocate*[1]. The High Court in a later decision[2] did not disapprove that test, but expressly 'preferred' the test of recklessness laid down in *Allan v Patterson*[3] which dealt with the meaning of recklessness in the offence of reckless driving under the Road Traffic Act 1972, s 2. It is here submitted that for a common law crime it is preferable to apply a common law standard of recklessness, and to avoid importing standards appropriate for statutory offences. After all, it was recognised by Lord Justice-General Clyde in *Quinn v Cunningham*[4] that Parliament introduced the statutory offence of reckless driving because of the high degree of culpability required to be proved in the common law crime.

1 1982 SCCR 152 at 155; see also *Quinn v Cunningham* 1956 JC 22.
2 *Gizzi v Tudhope* 1982 SCCR 442, 1983 SLT 214.
3 1980 SLT 77.
4 1956 JC 22.

1.32 It is criminal conduct culpably and recklessly to drive motor cars or other vehicles such as pedal cycles, or ride horses in a public place, to the danger of the lieges[1]. The culpable and reckless discharge of firearms[2] and throwing of bottles out of multi-storey flats[3] are criminal. The culpable and reckless supply of noxious substances to young persons is also criminal[4]. It is, however, unnecessary for actual injury to be sustained because the culpable and reckless endangering of the lieges is also criminal[5]. Such conduct not involving injury requires to reach the same high standard of criminal recklessness, but in practice where no actual injury results, it is more difficult for the Crown to prove the requisite standard of criminal recklessness.

1 *Macdonald* p 142.
2 *HM Advocate v Phipps* (1905) 4 Adam 616; *Gizzi v Tudhope* 1982 SCCR 442, 1983 SLT 214.
3 *R H W v HM Advocate* 1982 SCCR 152.
4 *Khaliq v HM Advocate* 1984 SLT 137. See Ferguson 'The Crime of Glue Sniffing—the Khaliq decision', 1984 SLT (News) 128.
5 *Gordon* paras 29–57 to 29–60.

1.33 In all of the cases dealing with reckless conduct, the question is not whether the accused actually recognised the existence of a risk and recklessly chose to take the chance of the risk materialising, but whether a reasonable man would have appreciated the risk and therefore would not have acted as the accused did. Accordingly, the question is in one sense not an issue relating to *mens rea* for it is not what the accused thought but what any reasonable man would have thought, but rather a question of negligence[1]. Thus, throughout the older reported decisions, the words 'negligence' and 'recklessness' are used interchangeably.

1 See P F 'Recklessness and the reasonable man in Scots Criminal Law', 1985 JR 29.

2. Murder

Homicide

2.01 Homicide is the destruction of a self-existent human life[1]. Suicide is not criminal; nor therefore is attempted suicide[2]. It is not homicide to 'kill' an unborn child. The beginning of human life is in law the drawing of breath[3]. It has not been authoritatively decided whether a child who has drawn breath but is not completely out of the body of its mother, is protected by the law of homicide[4], but it is highly likely that the Scottish courts would follow Macdonald[5] and hold that such a child could be killed and that its 'killer' could be convicted of murder or culpable homicide[6]. This seems to follow inevitably from the fact that it is clearly decided that where injuries are inflicted on a child *in utero* and the child is born alive but subsequently dies from the injuries, the person responsible can be convicted of common law homicide or of causing death by reckless driving contrary to s 1 of the Road Traffic Act 1988[7].

1 J H A Macdonald *The Criminal Law of Scotland* (5th edn, 1948) p 87.
2 G H Gordon *The Criminal Law of Scotland* (2nd edn, 1978) para 23.01.
3 *Macdonald* p 87.
4 *Gordon* para 23–02.
5 *Macdonald* p 87.
6 The crime of abortion being the wilful inducing of a miscarriage, does not provide for such a situation.
7 *McCluskey v HM Advocate* 1988 SCCR 629, applying *Kwok Chak Ming (No 1) v The Queen* [1963] HKLR 226, 349 (a case of manslaughter). *Hume* I, 187, considered that such a charge *might* be relevant.

2.02 The legal definition of death is not yet firmly settled but it is submitted that just as the drawing of breath is the beginning of life, so the termination of breathing should be the end of life. This was the underlying assumption in *Finlayson v HM Advocate*[1] where a man had been injected, with his consent, with a mixture of controlled drugs causing him to suffer irreversible brain damage. He was connected to a life-support machine in order that he could be artificially ventilated. The machine was eventually switched off and the accused was convicted of culpable homicide. The High Court rejected the argument

that it was the switching off which was the cause of death. The High Court had the opportunity but did not take it to hold that irreversible brain damage was the legal meaning of death.
1 1978 SLT (Notes) 60.

2.03 Leaving aside the statutory offence of causing death by reckless driving, homicide can be divided into three classes: murder, culpable homicide and non-criminal homicide[1].

Non-criminal homicide itself is susceptible of division into two classes: casual homicide and justifiable homicide.
1 *Macdonald* p 89; *Gordon* para 23–09.

2.04 Casual homicide is causing death by accident or pure misadventure[1]. Where a person while lawfully employed, kills unintentionally, neither meaning harm to anyone nor having failed in any duty to anyone, the law holds the death to be casual homicide[2].
1 *Hume* I, 194.
2 *Gordon* para 23–09.

2.05 Justifiable homicide is restricted to a few types of case[1], the principal example being killing in self-defence[2]. The other circumstances where homicide is justifiable are as follows[3]:
(1) The carrying out of the death sentence when lawfully imposed, and the passing of such a sentence, are justifiable homicide[4].
(2) Magistrates are entitled in the last resort[5], to use lethal force in the suppression of a riotous assembly[6]. However, Macdonald adds that the general rule is that 'where a mob commits, or threatens violence dangerous to life or property, the magistrate is bound to quell the riot, and where his authority is resisted, to maintain it by force'[7]. Whatever may have been the case in 1948 when this statement was written, it is extremely improbable that the courts would now hold homicide by a magistrate (or anyone acting on his orders) in defence of property to be justifiable[8].
(3) Members of Her Majesty's Armed Forces are justified in killing in the exercise of their duty[9]. Thus killing the enemy in time of war is not criminal. If a soldier is ordered by a magistrate to kill in suppressing a riot, the homicide is justifiable[10]. They are also entitled to rely on the defence of superior orders. The conditions for the invocation of the defence are stated by Hume:

'The order must be such as falls within the Officer's commission, and known line of duty; and though given in his own province, it must be at least an excusable order, or such as may be the subject of different opinions; *not a manifest injury and aggression on his part*[11].'

Thus killing on flagrantly illegal orders would not be justifiable.
(4) Sheriff Gordon notes that homicide is justifiable in cases of necessity other than self-defence but that there is no Scots authority on the matter[12]. It is here submitted that Scots law does not recognise a general defence of necessity and would therefore not hold homicide committed in necessitous circumstances to be justifiable[13].

1 *Macdonald* p 105.
2 See ch 8, below.
3 See *Gordon* paras 23–32 to 23–38.
4 *Hume* I, 195.
5 *Hume* I, 197.
6 *Macdonald* p 105.
7 *Macdonald* p 105.
8 *Macdonald* p 105. *Gordon* para 23–34 repeats Macdonald's view.
9 *Hume* I, 205; *Macdonald* p 106.
10 *Macdonald* p 105.
11 *Hume* I, 54 (emphasis added). See *HM Advocate v Hawton & Parker* (1861) 4 Irv 58 and *HM Advocate v Sheppard* 1941 JC 69.
12 *Gordon* para 23–37.
13 See ch 12, below.

Causation

2.06 Criminal homicide can be caused by either an act or an omission. An omission causing death will be criminal only if the accused was under a duty to act but failed to act. There are only two ways in which a duty can arise. First, the accused can come under a duty by reason of his relationship to the victim or his occupation. A father who stands by and watches his children drown[1] or starve to death[2] would be considered guilty of homicide in Scotland. A parent's duty to his children is a moral obligation which the law raises to a legal duty. It must, however, be doubted whether an adult son or daughter would come under a similar duty to his parents. Police officers have a duty to prevent crime and if a police officer were to stand by and watch a colleague assault a citizen, the police officer would be guilty art and part of assault by his failure to prevent it[3]. Secondly, an accused can by his own actings (which may, but need not, be criminal[4]) create a situation in which he is bound to act. Where it was alleged that an accused seriously assaulted a woman and therafter left her in a field 'in an injured and unconscious condition to the inclemency of the weather', Lord Mackay sustained the relevancy of the charge[5]. People do not otherwise incur criminal liability simply by failing to act. There is no general duty to act to assist someone or to prevent crime[6].

1 See *R v Russell* [1933] VLR 59.

2 See *R v Gibbins and Proctor* (1918) 13 Cr App Rep 134.
3 See *Macdonald* p 8; *Bonar v McLeod* 1983 SCCR 161.
4 See *MacPhail v Clark* 1983 SCCR 395.
5 *HM Advocate v McPhee* 1935 JC 46; see also *HM Advocate v McManimy & Higgins* (1847) Arkley 321; *Gordon* para 3–33.
6 *Gordon* para 3–32.

2.07 Death must be the direct result of the act or omission[1]. It is for the Crown to prove beyond reasonable doubt that death was the result of the criminal act or omission[2]. It is as criminal to kill a person suffering from a fatal disease as it is to kill the healthiest man[3]. To shorten a man's life by one second is criminal homicide: '[a] person dying is still in life, and may be killed'[4].

1 *Macdonald* p 87.
2 *Hendry v HM Advocate* 1988 SLT 25 'revising' *HM Advocate v McGinlay* 1983 SLT 562.
3 Hume I, 183; Alison *Principles* p 71, *Macdonald* pp 87–88; *Gordon* paras 4–22, 23–03.
4 As was said by Temple J in the Supreme Court of California in *People v Lewis* 124 Cal 551, 57 Pac (1899).

2.08 It is said by Macdonald that the injury inflicted must be 'real'[1] and he states that frightening a person so as to bring on a fever and cause death is not homicide. This view, perhaps as a result of the advances in medical science, cannot now be accepted. In *Bird v HM Advocate*[2], a woman who apparently had a weak heart, was pursued along a road and was caused such alarm that she collapsed and died of shock. The accused had pursued the woman because he had mistakenly formed the impression that the woman had stolen money from him. Lord Jamieson directed the jury that causing someone to die from emotional shock was criminal homicide. In his view he followed *HM Advocate v Brown*[3]:

'It was no defence at all that the victim was suffering from heart disease. Therefore, if they were of opinion that this woman died from the shock occasioned by the prisoner's criminal attempt to rob her, he was guilty . . . of culpable homicide.'

1 *Macdonald* p 87. See also Anderson *The Criminal Law of Scotland* p 145.
2 1952 JC 23.
3 (1879) 4 Coup 225 at 227.

2.09 Both *Bird* and *Brown* were concerned with shock following upon physical assault[1]. However in *Lourie v HM Advocate*[2] the Crown charged the accused with culpable homicide by entering uninvited the house of a 74-year-old woman who suffered from heart disease, and stealing her handbag in her presence as a result of which she was 'so alarmed and distressed that she then and there sustained a fatal heart attack' and died. No preliminary objection was stated to the relevancy

16 CAUSATION

of the libel but the convictions for culpable homicide were quashed on the ground that there was insufficient evidence to prove that the victim had observed the theft. It was conceded by the Crown that the allegations of uninvited entry and theft were crucial since they were the unlawful act causing death. While the court did not decide the relevancy of the indictment, it seems not unreasonable to expect that the court would have observed that the charge was irrelevant if they had considered it to be so,

1 As also in *Hendry v HM Advocate* 1988 SLT 25 where an assault upon a man who suffered from ischaemic heart disease and had been drinking and eating a heavy meal, also caused distress. See also *Taylor v HM Advocate* (June 1975, unreported), Court of Criminal Appeal.
2 1988 SCCR 634.

The 'thin skull' rule

2.10 It is irrelevant whether or not the accused knew that the victim suffered from a latent medical condition which made death result from the accused's act. The rule which the courts apply is that the accused must 'take his victim as he finds him'[1]. As Lord Justice-Clerk Cooper said:

'It is every whit as criminal to kill a feeble and infirm old man, or a new born infant as it is to kill an adult in the prime of life. However precarious the victim's hold on life may be, no person dare extinguish the spark by violent means but at his peril'[2].

1 *Gordon* para 4–21.
2 *HM Advocate v Robertson & Donoghue* (August 1975, unreported), High Court of Justiciary—see Gane and Stoddart *A Casebook on Scottish Criminal Law* (2nd edn, 1988) pp 183–184.

Novus actus interveniens

2.11 It is possible, however, for an accused whose act of violence has had effect on the victim, nonetheless to escape conviction if it can be shown that the actual cause of death was a supervening act or omission either on the part of the victim or of a third party. Such a supervening act is *novus actus interveniens*, a separate and subsequent cause of death. It becomes the actual cause of death because it comes after the injury inflicted by the accused. However, the test of whether there has occurred a *novus actus* is in Scots law a very demanding test. The test was provided in *Finlayson v HM Advocate*[1], where Lord Justice-General Emslie quoted with approval Lord Wright's dictum in *The Oropesa*[2]:

'To break the chain of causation it must be shown that there is something which I will cause ultroneous, something unwarrantable, a new cause which disturbs the sequence of events, something which can be described as either unreasonable or extraneous or extrinsic'[3].

Disconnecting a life-support machine where a victim was irreversibly brain-damaged was not an extraneous or extrinsic act, or unforeseeable or unforeseen[4].

1 1978 SLT (Notes) 60.
2 [1943] P 32.
3 The test was applied in *Khaliq v HM Advocate* 1984 SLT 137.
4 *Finlayson v HM Advocate* 1978 SLT (Notes) 60.

2.12 The act of suicide by a victim who is mortally injured, where the original wound inflicted by the accused was still an operating and substantial cause of the death, was held in the United States of America not to amount to a *novus actus*[1]. The Scottish courts would undoubtedly apply the same reasoning. Moreover, if it could be alleged and proved that the assault had induced suicide, the position would be just the same as occurred in *HM Advocate v Slaven*[2] where a woman who was the victim of an assault with intent to rape, fell over a cliff in an endeavour to escape from her assailants. The death was a consequence of the violent conduct of the accused. Equally, in England it was held that where a Jehovah's Witness, having been stabbed, refused on religious grounds to receive a blood transfusion which she knew would have saved her life, and died, the operative cause of death was the stabbing[3]. The decision was simply an application of the rule that one must take one's victim as one finds him and this means the whole man, not just the physical man.

1 See *People v Lewis* 124 Cal 551, 57 Pac (1899).
2 (1885) 5 Coup 694. See *Macdonald* p 100.
3 *R v Blaue* [1975] 3 All ER 446.

2.13 Malregimen is the term applied to circumstances in which a person dies as a consequence of bad medical treatment for injuries sustained as a result of criminal conduct. Incompetent medical treatment may break the causal chain. If a wound would not have proved fatal but for the flagrantly incompetent treatment which followed on it, the wound cannot be the cause of death[1]. The general rule, however, is that negligent treatment following upon a mortal injury is irrelevant[2]. The logic of this view is irresistible since it would never do to allow every criticism that could be made of the treatment after the wound was received, to furnish a ground for acquittal. If a wound is not going to be fatal in itself, different considerations apply although if the courts could affirm that the original wound played a substantial part in, or was a major contribution to, the death, the original wound would be held to be the cause of death. To avoid liability the subsequent treatment would require to be ultroneous, unforeseeable and unforeseen[3].

1 See *HM Advocate v Williamson* (1866) 5 Irv 326; Macdonald p 88.
2 *Gordon* para 4–37.
3 See *Finlayson v HM Advocate* 1978 SLT (Notes) 60.

Murder

2.14 The classical definition of murder is provided by Macdonald: 'Murder is constituted by any wilful act causing the destruction of life, whether intended to kill, or displaying such wicked recklessness as to imply a disposition depraved enough to be regardless of consequences'[1]. This definition has been accepted over the years in various forms. Lord Sands in *HM Advocate v Fraser and Rollins*[2] told the jury: 'You do not require the deliberate intention to kill, but you must have reckless use of force without any consideration of what the results of that use of force may be'. Most importantly, in the leading decision of the Court of Criminal Appeal, *Cawthorne v HM Advocate*[3], Lord Justice-General Clyde accepted Macdonald's statement of the *mens rea* which is essential to the establishment of the common law crime of murder.

1 *Macdonald* p 89.
2 1923 JC 60.
3 1968 JC 32.

2.15 In *Cawthorne*, the trial judge had directed the jury that there were three possible mental states sufficient to found a charge of murder: intent to kill, wicked recklessness and intent to do bodily harm. The issue in *Cawthorne* was whether the trial judge was correct in refusing to direct the jury that for the accused to be guilty of attempted murder he had to have possessed a deliberate intention to kill when he discharged several shots from a rifle into a room in which people had barricaded themselves. The trial judge told the jury what the definition of murder was, and thereafter directed that if any of these mental states was displayed by the accused but the victim did not die, the crime was attempted murder. The essence of the appeal was accordingly that the trial judge had introduced the concept of a reckless attempt into Scots Law. As a matter of logic, of course, it is impossible to describe an attempt as anything other than an intentional act.

2.16 The Court of Criminal Appeal in *Cawthorne* was not, therefore, concerned with the question whether or not the three mental states could each satisfy the definition of murder. While the point may have been conceded[1], the court did not hold that apart from an intention to kill and wicked recklessness, there was a third *mens rea* for murder, namely intention to do serious (or grievous) bodily harm. However, juries are sometimes charged to that effect. Lord Sutherland, for example, in *HM Advocate v Hartley*[2] directed that an intentional act causing the destruction of life 'either with the intent to kill or cause serious bodily harm' was one branch of the *mens rea* of murder. It is, however, arguable that an intention to do any degree of harm falling short of fatal harm cannot be a sufficient intention for murder. However, if A intends to inflict serious bodily harm on B and in fact kills B, A may be guilty of murder by reason of his wicked recklessness[3].

1 See *Gordon* para 23–20.
2 1989 SLT 135.
3 See *Macdonald* p 91.

2.17 Wicked recklessness is simply recklessness of such a gross type that it deserves to be stigmatised as murder[1].

'If you act in such a way as to show that you don't really care whether the person you are attacking lives or dies, then that can constitute this degree of wicked recklessness which is required to constitute murder. It may, in the end of the day come as a considerable suprise to you, and indeed a matter of regret too that your victim dies, but that doesn't alter the fact that you have committed murder'[2].

Recklessness is objectively assessed. It is not a question whether the accused knew of the risk of death and carried on regardless, but whether a reasonable man would have known of the risk. What the accused knew is irrelevant (although the courts never expressly state that). Hence the victim's death can be a surprise to the accused who is nonetheless guilty of murder.

1 *Gordon* para 23–19.
2 *HM Advocate v Hartley* 1989 SLT 135 at 136.

Determining the mental state

2.18 If an accused declares that he wishes to kill A and assaults A in consequence of which A dies, the jury has no difficulty where appropriate, in concluding that the death was murder. An intention to kill B is evidenced. However, it is necessary in most cases to infer the intention or recklessness from the circumstances of the death. The type of weapon used (if any), the number of blows inflicted and the type of injuries which the victim sustained are only some of the factors which the jury are encouraged by the judge to take into account in assessing the mental state of the accused. In a well-known passage, Lord Justice-Clerk Aitchison told the jury:

'People who use knives and pokers and hatchets against a fellow citizen are not entitled to say "we did not mean to kill", if death results. If people resort to the use of deadly weapons of this kind, they are guilty of murder, whether or not they intended to kill'[1].

As has been observed[2] this suggests that the use of a lethal weapon in itself makes the crime murder. This cannot be the case although the use of a lethal weapon, and the fact that the lethal weapon used was carried by the accused before the assault, are important factors in determining the attitude of the accused to the possibility of death resulting from his actions.

1 *HM Advocate v McGuinness* 1937 JC 37 at 40.
2 *Gordon* para 23–21.

Homicide in the course of robbery

2.19 As a general rule it is not murder simply because homicide is committed in the course of the commission of some other crime. Writers such as Hume and Alison, for example, considered that death caused by the carrying out of criminal abortion, was always murder[1]. Homicide resulting from rape and fire-raising was also recognised by some as always constituting murder[2]. These views were the result of a highly objective view of the mental element in crime, and flowed from the notion of dole, or general wickedness, which was (and indeed to a certain extent, still is) the basis of Scots criminal law. With one exception these cases of 'constructive murder' do not now receive recognition by the courts.

1 *Hume* I, 264; Alison *Principles* p 52. See also *Gordon* para 23–28.
2 See *Gordon* paras 23–29 and 23–30.

2.20 The one exception is the case of homicide in the course of robbery. In *HM Advocate v Miller and Denovan*[1] Lord Wheatley (as he then was) directed the jury that in robbery where violence is used and the victim dies, if it is homicide then it must be murder. On appeal the High Court approved the direction. The existence of this exception was reaffirmed in *Melvin v HM Advocate*[2] where the High Court held that the jury was entitled to return a discriminating verdict, convicting one accused of murder and the other of culpable homicide, 'in a case where intent to kill was not suggested or established or indeed any antecedent concerted intention to carry out an assault and robbery on the deceased or any other person'[3]. There is no logical reason for the continued existence of this exception save the public policy consideration (which had more relevance in the days of capital punishment), that robbers who commit homicide deserve to be convicted of murder.

1 (November 1960, unreported), High Court of Justiciary. See *Gordon* para 23–26.
2 1984 SCCR 113. See also *Malone v HM Advocate* 1988 SCCR 498.
3 *Melvin v HM Advocate* 1984 SCCR 113 at 117.

3. Culpable homicide

3.01 Culpable homicide may be divided into two distinct categories. First, there is voluntary culpable homicide which is homicide commited in particular circumstances which the law holds to be sufficient to reduce the crime from murder to culpable homicide. It is in effect murder under mitigating circumstances[1]. Secondly, there is involuntary culpable homicide which is 'the causing of death by any unlawful act'[2].

1 G H Gordon *The Criminal Law of Scotland* (2nd edn, 1978), ch 25.
2 *HM Advocate v Hartley* 1989 SLT 135 at 136.

Voluntary culpable homicide

3.02 A charge of murder will be reduced to culpable homicide in circumstances demonstrating that the killer acted under provocation[1] or while he was suffering from diminished responsibility[2]. It is also, however, the practice for the Crown not to charge certain homicides as murder. The following cases are given by Sheriff Gordon[3] as the 'unofficial categories' of culpable homicide: (1) the killing by a mother of her child within one year of birth; (2) killing someone who is dying in extreme pain, in order to end the patient's suffering; (3) the killing in furtherance of a 'suicide pact'; (4) killing under necessity or coercion; (5) killing by a member of Her Majesty's Armed Forces in excess of his duty such as when excessive violence is used; and (6) killing by 'pure omission', for example, causing the death of a child by neglect or desertion.

1 See ch 9, below.
2 See ch 10, below.
3 See *Gordon* paras 25–02 to 25–07.

Involuntary culpable homicide

3.03 It is unwise to attempt to provide too specific an analysis of the categories of involuntary culpable homicide because of the wide spectrum of varying degrees of moral culpability which the crime encompasses. However, it can be said that broadly speaking, there are two species of involuntary culpable homicide. First, if a person commits a crime, usually but not always assault, and a death results then the crime is culpable homicide. Secondly, a person may be engaged in a perfectly lawful course of conduct but by gross negligence he causes the death of another. The degree of carelessness (or as it is sometimes called, recklessness) is important because it is not mere negligence in the ordinary civil sense that will found a charge of culpable homicide.

Homicide as a result of another crime

3.04 Any assault which causes death is at the very least culpable homicide. In *McDermott v HM Advocate*[1], the Court of Criminal Appeal stated the law thus:

'Homicide is the killing of another, and where death is brought about by an unlawful act, including assault upon the victim, it is always homicide and it is always culpable'[2].

As Lord Moncrieff said in *HM Advocate v Delaney*[3]:

'If a man takes life in circumstances which infer criminal responsibility ... it is in all cases for the death that he is responsible'.

This statement was quoted with approval in *McDermott*. The accused will only escape a conviction for culpable homicide if it cannot be proved that the accused's acts caused death.

1 1974 SLT 206.
2 *McDermott v HM Advocate* 1974 SLT 206 overruled *Gilmour v HM Advocate* 1938 SLT 72 and *McCluskey v HM Advocate* 1959 SLT 215.
3 1946 SLT 25.

3.05 Thus any assault which leads to death is at least culpable homicide. The assault need not be more than trivial. A punch on the chin which causes a man to stumble backwards, catch his heel on the kerb, fall over and fracture his skull leading to death, is culpable homicide[1]. To spit at someone causing him to take evasive action and fall, thereby sustaining fatal injuries is culpable homicide. Any technical assault leading directly to the victim's death is culpable homicide[2]. The death of the victim need not be foreseeable or foreseen, far less intended or desired. Thus, it is just as much culpable homicide to assault a person who appears to be healthy but has a weak or diseased heart unknown to the accused, as it is to assault an invalid. This is an application of the rule that one takes one's victim as he actually is and not simply as he appears to be³. The distinction between assaulting an old man who dies and an apparently healthy man who dies because of a latent defect such as a diseased heart, is recognised only in sentence where assault on an old man would normally attract a higher penalty.

1 See *HM Advocate v Hartley* 1989 SLT 135.
2 See *Bird v HM Advocate* 1952 JC 23.
3 See *Gordon* para 26–17 where the failure to observe the distinction between the patent and latent medical disabilities is criticised.

3.06 Culpable homicide can also result from other crimes not involving assault or violence¹. It is culpable homicide to desert a child even in circumstances of no apparent danger, if the child dies as a result of the desertion². A person who culpably and recklessly sets fire to paint at the rear of a building occupied by elderly residents some of whom die as a consequence, is guilty of culpable homicide³. Malicious mischief to a motor car the brakes of which fail to operate as a result of the damage, is sufficient basis for a conviction for culpable homicide. In short, any criminal act causing death is sufficient for culpable homicide. The consequence of the act need not be foreseen. In *Mowles v HM Advocate*⁴ the accused reasonably believing that a shotgun was unloaded, pointed the shotgun at a man in order to get him to leave a house. The weapon could not be discharged by trigger pressure but could accidentally discharge if knocked or dropped. The weapon discharged when it was grabbed by the barrel, thereby killing an occupant of the house. The accused pled guilty to culpable homicide and was sentenced to five years' imprisonment. The sentence was reduced to six months' imprisonment on appeal because (1) the accused was ignorant of the fact that the weapon was loaded and (2) he held on reasonable grounds a positive belief that the weapon was unloaded. These factors could not prevent the crime being culpable homicide because there was an initial assault, but they did affect the penalty for the crime.

1 See *Lourie v HM Advocate* 1988 SCCR 634.
2 *Macdonald* p 98.
3 See *Mathieson v HM Advocate* 1981 SCCR 196.
4 1986 SCCR 117.

3.07 The distinction between murder and culpable homicide is in some cases very obvious and in others, somewhat blurred. Slapping someone so that he falls and dies is clearly culpable homicide because there is no intention to kill (or to do grievous bodily harm¹) and there is no wicked recklessness inferring a disposition depraved enough to be regardless of whether the victim lives or dies. The distinction between murder and culpable homicide only arises in cases where there is no intention to kill but merely recklessness. The question is then, what degree of recklessness was present in the accused's actings? If, for example, A and B are engaged in an assault involving kicking the victim on the head, and punching and kicking him on his face, it is difficult to distinguish between A and B's conduct where there is no intention to kill. Their recklessness must be equal and they should be convicted of murder or culpable homicide unless there are striking differences in the relevant conduct of each of A and B². The distinction between the degree of recklessness sufficient for culpable homicide but insufficient for murder is accordingly ineffable. Juries can only be told that if they do not consider that the accused's actings although criminal, were so wickedly reckless, then they can convict of culpable homicide.

1 See paras 2.15 and 2.16, above.
2 See *Malone v HM Advocate* 1988 SCCR 498 at 508, applying Lord Avonside's observation in *Melvin v HM Advocate* 1984 SCCR 113.

Lawful act homicide

3.08 The second category of involuntary culpable homicide occurs when A by sheer gross negligence, fails to discharge a duty properly and thereby causes the death of B. Macdonald says:

'Culpable homicide may result from neglect of proper precautions, or of moderation in the doing of what is legal, or from general carelessness and neglect of duty'¹.

There is no initial or preliminary criminal act such as assault involved. The crime of culpable homicide is constituted in these circumstances by the degree of negligence on the part of the accused. In the ultimate it is a question of moral blameworthiness. Not every degree of blame is sufficient². Fault or *culpa* which would be sufficient for civil liability is insufficient for culpable homicide.

1 Macdonald p 100.
2 Macdonald p 100; *Paton v HM Advocate* 1935 JC 19.

3.09 The requisite standard of recklessness is provided by Lord Justice-Clerk Aitchison in *Paton v HM Advocate*¹:

'At one time the rule of law was that any blame was sufficient, where death resulted, to justify a verdict of guilty of culpable homicide. Unfortunately, this law has to some extent been modified by decisions of the Court, and it is now necessary to show gross, or wicked, or criminal negligence, something amounting to, or at any rate analogous, to a criminal indifference to consequences, before a jury can find culpable homicide proved'.

Although the Lord Justice-Clerk considered the standard to be too high, the standard is still that provided by him in *Paton*. The expression 'negligence' is used as a synonym for 'recklessness' because Scots law makes no distinction between A who recognises the risk of injury or death, and runs it causing death, and B who does not appreciate the risk but ought to have done so. The accused is guilty of culpable homicide if a reasonable man would consider that the accused displayed gross negligence in what he did.

1 1935 JC 19.

3.10 The difficulty with the vague definition of recklessness or gross negligence which constitutes the crime of culpable homicide is that there is a statutory form of criminal homicide. Section 1 of the Road Traffic Act 1988 provides that a person who causes the death of another person by driving a motor vehicle recklessly, is guilty of an offence[1]. The meaning of recklessness in the 1972 Act has been stated by the High Court in *Allan v Patterson*[2]:

'Judges and juries will readily understand, and juries might well be reminded, that before they can apply the adverb "recklessly" to the driving in question they must find that it fell far below the standard of driving expected of the competent and careful driver and that it occurred either in the face of obvious and material dangers which were or should have been observed, appreciated and guarded against, or in circumstances which showed a complete disregard for any potential dangers which might result from the way in which the vehicle was being driven'.

1 The person can be injured *in utero* so long as death resulting from the injuries occurs after birth: see *McCluskey v HM Advocate* 1988 SCCR 629.
2 1980 SLT 77.

3.11 Since the meaning of recklessness in *Allan v Patterson* has been unreservedly accepted by the High Court for common law crimes involving recklessness[1], it is evident that there is no good reason for excluding culpable homicide from that class of crimes involving *Allan v Patterson* recklessness. Accordingly, what is the distinction between culpable homicide and a contravention of s 1 of the Road Traffic Act 1988? The answer, though unsatisfactory, is provided in *Dunn v HM Advocate*[2] and amounts to this—if a jury considers that the reckless driving in question was so serious or gross a variety of recklessness, the crime should be culpable homicide. The distinction between culpable homicide and the statutory offence is therefore an emotional one. The jury requires to decide the question on an evaluation of blameworthiness[3].

1 *Gizzi v Tudhope* 1982 SCCR 442, 1983 SLT 214; see ch 1, para 1.31, above.
2 1960 JC 55.

3 See also *R v Seymour* [1983] 2 AC 493.

3.12 This problem is a real one because it is not uncommon for the Crown to charge an accused with culpable homicide or alternatively, a contravention of s 1[1]. If the *mens rea* of both crimes is the same (ie, *Allan v Patterson* recklessness), the result is that the jury assumes the role of sentencer. The maximum period of imprisonment for the statutory offence is five years but the maximum term for culpable homicide is life imprisonment. The jury in effect is required to decide whether the driving was so bad as to merit the accused being imprisoned for more than five years.

1 Road Traffic Act 1972, s 1 (as amended) (now the Road Traffic Act 1988, s 1).

Attempted homicide

3.13 While there is a well recognised crime of attempted murder, there is no such crime of attempted culpable homicide. If an accused is convicted of attempted murder in mitigating circumstances involving provocation or diminished responsibility, the appropriate conviction for the jury to return is assault under provocation[1] or assault on the ground of diminished responsibility[2].

1 *Brady v HM Advocate* 1986 SCCR 191.
2 *HM Advocate v Blake* 1986 SLT 661.

4. Rape

4.01 Rape is the carnal knowledge of a woman forcibly and against her will[1]. It is a distinct offence and is not merely an aggravated form of assault[2]. The crime can be committed only by a male acting as the principal, although a woman can be art and part in the crime. A female accomplice, for example, becomes guilty by giving assistance to the male assailant, restraining the victim, and stifling the victim's calls for help. A husband may be guilty of raping his wife whether or not he is living with her[3]. There is no such thing as implied consent to sexual intercourse (revocable or otherwise) arising out of the fact of marriage[4]. A prostitute can be raped but the proof of the crime may in certain circumstances be more difficult. The law is now as Lord Justice-Clerk Macdonald said in 1897:

'Every woman is entitled to protection from attack upon her person. Even a prostitute may be held to be ravished if the proof establishes a rape, although she may admit that she is a prostitute'[5].

1 Hume *Commentaries*, I, 301; Alison *Principles* p 209; J H A Macdonald *The Criminal Law of Scotland* (5th edn, 1948) p 119; G H Gordon *The Criminal Law of Scotland* (2nd edn, 1978) para 33–01. See also *HM Advocate v Grainger and Rae* 1932 JC 40 and *S v HM Advocate* 1989 SLT 469.
2 Cf *S v HM Advocate* 1989 SLT 469 and *Report on Evidence in Cases of Rape and Other Sexual Offences* (Scot Law Com no 78 (21.7.83), para 2.1).
3 *S v HM Advocate* 1989 SLT 469.
4 See *HM Advocate v D* 1982 SCCR 182 and *HM Advocate v Paxton* 1985 SLT 96, which must now, however, be read in the light of *S v HM Advocate*.
5 *Dickie v HM Advocate* (1897) 2 Adam 331 p 337. This proposition ironically was more widely stated than the law in 1897 permitted.

4.02 For rape to be established it is essential that the Crown prove: (1) that the victim was a woman who did not consent to sexual intercourse, and (2) that the accused knew that she did not consent or if he did not, that he did not have a genuine belief that she did consent.

4.03 It is not rape for a man to have forcible anal or oral intercourse with a female victim. Such an offence is indecent assault. Equally a male person cannot be raped by another man, or by a woman. Penetration of the vagina is essential for rape but it need not be complete penetration¹ and it can be to any extent. There need not be emission². There is no presumption or rule that a boy under the age of puberty (14 years of age) cannot in law commit rape. Macdonald observes: 'It is a question of proof, not of theory'³. A boy aged 13 years and 10 months was convicted of rape⁴.

1 *Macdonald* p 120.
2 *Gordon* para 33–02.
3 *Macdonald* p 121.
4 *Robert Fulton, Junior* (1841) 2 Swin 564.

Consent

4.04 In *Meek v HM Advocate*¹ the Court of Criminal Appeal held that it was a defence to a charge of rape that the accused honestly believed that the woman was consenting when she was not, even though such belief was not held on reasonable grounds. As the criminal intent in the crime of rape is to force intercourse upon a woman against her will, if an accused believes no matter how unreasonably that the victim was consenting, he cannot properly be convicted of rape².

1 1982 SCCR 613.
2 See also *R v Morgan* [1976] AC 182.

4.05 The decision in *Meek* does not, however, mean that an accused can be easily and wrongly acquitted. Lord Justice-General Emslie in *Meek* said: 'The absence of reasonable grounds for such an alleged belief will, however, have a considerable bearing upon whether any jury will accept such an "honest belief" was held', and, as *Meek* makes plain, failure to give such a direction to the jury will not necessarily result in the conviction being quashed. Where there is one account of sexual intercourse violently forced upon an unwilling victim and a competing account of an honest belief in consent, there is no 'half-way house' and a trial judge is under no obligation to give such a direction¹.

1 See Ferguson 'Rape and reasonable belief' 1983 SLT (News) 89. See also *Quinn v HM Advocate* 1990 SCCR 254.

4.06 Moreover, it does not follow from *Meek* that a man who has sexual intercourse while not caring whether or not his victim consents, is guilty of rape. However, it is submitted here that there is no good reason why he should not be convicted of rape. There is no authority upon the point. If, however, rape can be committed both recklessly or intentionally, the court will face the same dilemma as arose in *Cawthorne v HM Advocate*¹, namely, can a person who is only reckless whether or not his victim consents, be convicted of attempted rape. It is vital that if the question arises the Scottish courts will give the same answer as they did in *Cawthorne* in the case of murder, and hold that attempted rape can be committed recklessly.

1 1968 JC 32.

The use of force

4.07 Many rapes are committed by the use of force, sometimes considerable and violent force, in order to overcome the resistance of the victim. Macdonald, Hume and Alison[1] required that rape be committed forcibly and against the will of the victim. This double requirement is not now necessary. All that is necessary is that the victim did not consent to sexual intercourse. No doubt the victim will ordinarily offer resistance, but the absence of signs of violence having been used does not preclude a conviction for rape. A woman's will may be overcome by mere threats of deadly violence, by the use of a knife or other weapon, or indeed by threats of violence to other persons such as children. The significance of resistance is only as evidence of the victim's lack of consent[2].

1 *Macdonald* p 119; *Hume* I, 302; Alison *Principles* p 209.
2 See *Barbour v HM Advocate* 1982 SCCR 195 at 198 per Lord Stewart in his charge to the jury.

Absence of force

4.08 Since absence of consent is of the essence of the crime of rape, it is not rape for a man to have intercourse with a sleeping woman. The court in *HM Advocate v Charles Sweenie*[1] held that such conduct was a form of indecent assault but could not be rape because force was absent. However, it seems clear that since the victim was asleep and could neither give not withhold her consent, the correct view should have been that the crime was rape. Sheriff Gordon explains the decision on the basis of the unwillingness to 'extend' the scope of what was then a capital crime[2], and this was no doubt the prime reason for the court's decision. However, since such an accused could not genuinely believe that the victim was consenting to sexual intercourse and at most he could believe that she would consent if given the choice, he should therefore have been guilty of recklessly committing rape. But, as has already been observed, reckless rape is not yet formally acknowledged to exist in the law of Scotland.

1 (1858) 3 Irv 109.
2 *Gordon* para 33–06.

4.09 It was not rape at common law for A to have sexual intercourse with B by pretending to be C, B's husband: *HM Advocate v Fraser*¹. However, such conduct was deemed to be rape by s 4 of the Criminal Law Amendment Act 1885 which is now s 2(2) of the Sexual Offences (Scotland) Act 1976. It is moreover rape in terms of the 1976 Act for a man to pretend to be the victim's first husband who is believed by the victim to be dead, notwithstanding that she subsequently remarried².

1 (1847) Arkley 280.
2 *HM Advocate v Montgomery* 1926 JC 2.

4.10 If the victim is drugged so as to overcome her will, the crime is rape. Lord Justice-Clerk Aitchison directed the jury in *HM Advocate v Logan*¹:

'If you thought that the Crown had proved that the woman was plied with drink, and drink of a deadly kind, the nature of which was concealed from her, in order to overcome her resistance, you could find a verdict of guilty of rape'.

However, his Lordship further directed that if the victim took the drink of her own free will, 'it had not been given from a criminal purpose', and had found advantage was taken of her while she was insensible, the crime would not be rape but indecent assault². The Lord Justice-Clerk observed that this was perhaps a very odd distinction but that it was required by the decision of the Court in *HM Advocate v Charles Sweenie*³. However that may be, there is an illogicality in the distinction since there can be no indecent assault if the victim consents just as surely as consent precludes rape. Clearly the court in *Sweenie*³ had to penalise such conduct and indecent assault was the only crime available for that purpose.

1 1935 JC 100.
2 See also *Sweeney v X* 1982 SCCR 509.
3 *HM Advocate v Charles Sweenie* (1858) 3 Irv 109.

Girls legally incapable of consent

4.11 Where the victim is a girl who is under the age of puberty (12 years of age), it is rape for a man to have sexual intercourse with her and the absence of consent need not be proved because she is held in the eyes of the law to be incapable of consent¹. Moreover, Parliament has intervened and by s 3(1) of the Sexual Offences (Scotland) Act 1976 it is provided that any person who has unlawful[2] sexual intercourse with any girl under the age of 13 years commits an offence, the maximum punishment of which is life imprisonment. Section 3(2) provides that an attempt at such a crime is punishable by no more than two years' imprisonment[3]. While no doubt it would be necessary for the Crown to prove some form of dole or *mens rea* in seeking a conviction at common law, s 3 makes no reference to, and involves no implication that there must be, a particular mental element in the contravention of this statute. Thus, at common law the Crown would require to establish that the accused knew or ought to have known that the victim was under 12 years of age, but would not require to do so when proceeding under the 1976 Act[4]. Since by virtue of s 13 of the 1976 Act, a jury is entitled on a charge of rape to convict an accused of a contravention of s 3 of the 1976 Act, no real difficulty now arises out of what is in any event a speculative distinction.

1 *Hume* I, 303; Alison *Principles* p 213; *Macdonald* p 119.
2 Ie extra-marital; see *Gordon* para 33–18.
3 Ie when the case is tried on indictment; when tried summarily, the maximum penalty is three months' imprisonment.
4 See *Gordon* para 33–15.

Mentally deficient or mentally ill women

4.12 It was never decided at common law whether it was rape for a man to have sexual intercourse with a mentally deficient or mentally ill woman[1]. Macdonald suggested that an idiot would probably be held to be incapable of consent, and so intercourse with her would be rape[2]. Macdonald did not, however, deal with the question of a person who was incapable of consent by reason of mental illness[3]. Certainly it is clear that Parliament did not consider that there was any rule which held that mentally deficient women were incapable in law of consenting to sexual intercourse[4]. It is unclear whether persons who have sexual intercourse with mentally ill women are guilty of rape or indeed of any common law crime at all[5].

1 *Gordon* para 33–15.
2 *Macdonald* p 119. See *HM Advocate v Grainger and Rae* 1932 JC 40 at p 41; 'the idiot has, in law and in fact, no will' (Lord Anderson).
3 *Macdonald* p 119.
4 See *Gordon* para 33–16; Criminal Law Amendment Act 1885, s 5(2).
5 See *Mack v HM Advocate* 1959 SLT 288 where Lord Thompson observed that it was not a crime to have intercourse with a certified lunatic.

Clandestine injury to women[1]

4.13 There is a category of unlawful sexual intercourse which is not rape but is struck at by the common law. Macdonald describes the crime of 'clandestine injury to women' which is committed when sexual intercourse is had with a woman who is insensible through sleep, a fit, drink or the like 'so that she neither yields nor withholds consent'[2]. Macdonald describes the offence as an assault aggravated by indecency and real injury to the person[3].

1 *Gordon* para 33–21.
2 *Macdonald* p 120.
3 See para 4.10, above.

5. Robbery

5.01 The crime of robbery is theft perpetrated by means of actual personal violence or by threats of immediate violence[1]. Robbery is related to the crime of theft but is a separate crime from it. There can be no robbery without theft. Thus, since it is not theft for a man to steal his own property in the belief that it is the property of another, similarly it would not be robbery for a man to use violence against another in order to take his own property. The violence would however be generally punishable as an assault.

1 See G H Gordon *The Criminal Law of Scotland* (2nd edn, 1978) para 16–01.

Mens rea

5.02 Since theft is the basis of the crime of robbery it follows that the intention in theft must also be proved in robbery. Macdonald states that there must be an intention to appropriate another person's property[1]. It has been authoritatively determined by the High Court that an intention permanently to deprive the owner of his property, while it was formerly the law, is now not necessary for the commission of theft. An intention temporarily to deprive the owner of his property will now be sufficient *mens rea* for theft[2]. Thus, if A, intending only to take a motor cycle for a run and thereafter to return it, used violence against its owner to secure the use of the motor cycle, the crime would now be robbery. The property taken need not, however, be owned by the victim of the robbery. The victim need only have custody or charge of the property which his assailant appropriates[3]. Furthermore, it is open to doubt whether the custody of the property need be lawful. If A assaults B, who is a thief, in order to deprive B of stolen goods, the courts would be likely to hold that A had committed robbery unless, of course, the violence used was reasonable in the circumstances and was used in order to prevent crime and not for A's own gain.

1 J H A Macdonald *The Criminal Law of Scotland* (5th edn, 1948) p 41.
2 See *Milne v Tudhope* 1981 SLT (Notes) 42; *Grant v Allan* 1988 SLT 11.
3 Hume *Commentaries* I, 106.

Robbery and assault distinguished

5.03 Robbery also requires the proof of violence, or at least that theft was achieved by the use of threats of immediate physical violence. However, the violence need not be considerable. Hume stated the law in the following terms:

'There may be a robbery without any wounding or beating of the person (and when such violence is used, it may therefore be libelled as an accusation . . .); and without any forcible wresting or tearing of the thing from the person; or even any sort of endeavour on the part of the sufferer to detain it'[1].

The law accordingly gives a wide latitude to the concept of violence. The distinction which Hume attempted to draw was between, on the one hand, theft by surprise where the stolen article is taken without the victim being frightened in any way, or being allowed time to resist the theft as in the case of picking pockets, and, on the other hand, any theft which did involve immediate alarm, or a scuffle or a resistance of any sort such as occurs in the case of 'mugging'.

1 *Hume* I, 106.

5.04 Robbery is a separate crime. While there cannot be robbery without an assault, robbery is not simply an aggravation of theft[1]. However, the usual style of charge is that A 'did assault B . . . and did rob him of . . .'. This is because the typical case is where B is assaulted by being punched or pushed, and his wallet or other valuables are then taken from him. This is properly termed a charge of assault and robbery, which as Hume explained is robbery aggravated by the preceding assault. It is, however, possible for the charge to libel simply that A 'did rob B of . . .'. This style of charge is uncommon, but justified when, as Sheriff Gordon states, '[t]he taking is not preceded by any assault, but is itself so violent as to constitute robbery'[2]. In *Cromar v HM Advocate*[3], for example, the accused came up behind his victim and pulled at a bag which the victim was holding. The victim attempted to hold on to the bag but the plastic handle on the bag snapped and the accused made off with the bag. The accused was convicted of robbery under deletion of a specific libel of assault. The High Court affirmed the jury's verdict. Lord Justice-Clerk Ross stated the opinion of the Court that '[t]here was in that description of the events sufficient to entitle the jury to reach the conclusion that the theft had been accomplished by means of personal violence and that, accordingly, this was robbery and not theft'[4].

However, given that robbery only requires proof of violence and not necessarily assault, the distinction between theft and robbery can be difficult to discern. The only judicial statement on the issue was given by Lord Justice-Clerk Aitchison in *O'Neill v HM Advocate*[5]. Lord Justice-Clerk Aitchison said:

'The answer to the question thus raised depends upon what is the true legal definition of robbery. It is well settled that in robbery there must be violence. On the other hand, it is not necessary to robbery that there should be actual physical assault. It is enough if the degree of force used can reasonably be described as violence'[6].

1 Alison *Principles* p 227; *Gordon* para 16–13.
2 *Gordon* para 16–10.
3 1987 SCCR 635.
4 1987 SCCR 635 at 637.
5 1934 JC 98.
6 See also *HM Advocate v Fegen* (1838) 2 Swin 25.

5.05 Robbery is violence or assault committed with the intention of committing theft. Logically, the violence must therefore precede the theft. If A takes a bag from B and B attempts to retrieve the bag, causing A to assault B to ward him off, it is not robbery[1] because in these circumstances the theft would have been completed before the violence was committed and accordingly the violence could not have been committed with the ulterior intention of committing theft.

1 See *Gordon* para 16–07.

Threats and intimidation

5.06 Threats of personal violence are sufficient to constitute robbery but only if they are threats of immediate violence to the person from whom the robber removes the property. There does not need to be actual physical violence. The essence of robbery is the overcoming of the victim's will to retain his property. If A threatens B that he will shoot B if B does not give him his money, the crime is robbery. It is not necessary for A to present a gun at B, which in any event would amount to an assault. However, the crime is not robbery but extortion if A threatened to kill B in seven days' time if by that time B has not paid money to A. Extortion is blackmail, and need not involve threats of personal violence. More importantly, extortion is not concerned with threats of immediate harm[1].

1 See *Gordon* para 21–02.

5.07 Finally, it should be noted that it is doubtful whether a threat to inflict immediate physical injury on a person other than the person who is thereby induced to hand over money or other valuables, is robbery. If A says to B that he will kill B's wife or child if B does not immediately give him money, the Scottish courts would undoubtedly punish the threat as criminal but such circumstances do not amount to robbery. The violence which is threatened is not threatened against the possessor of the goods and accordingly cannot give rise to a charge of robbery. It would be theft committed in aggravated circumstances. Equally, if the threat of immediate harm does not involve physical harm, then the crime should not be robbery. Sheriff Gordon[1] however suggests that if A picks up B's telephone and threatens that he will inform the police or even the press of something detrimental to B unless B hands over a sum of money, A is guilty of robbing B of the money. While there is consistency in this approach since the essence of robbery is the overcoming of the victim's resistance to parting with his property, and in these circumstances it should not matter how the resistance is overcome, there is nonetheless no clear institutional or other authority for Sheriff Gordon's view. Indeed, the only discussion of robbery by the institutional writers relate to violence and threats of violence[2]. It is submitted, therefore, that robbery based on threats of violence is limited to cases in which the violence is physical. A false accusation of crime made to the police would be criminal but a threat of it cannot be robbery even if it induces the victim to part with his possessions. Macdonald states that 'violent conduct, producing reasonable fear of coercion or bodily injury... is sufficient to constitute the offence'[3]. It is here suggested that that statement is restrictive of the law's concept of violence as constituting robbery.

1 *Gordon* para 16–13.
2 See *Hume* I, 108; Alison *Principles* p 231.
3 *Macdonald* p 40.

Piracy

5.08 At common law robbery committed on the high seas was punished as the specific crime of piracy. Macdonald defined piracy as being 'hostile depredations committed on the seas, without a commission from any state to authorise them'[1]. However, if the sovereign, for example, authorised the capture of enemy ships in time of war, the act was one of privateering, and not piracy[2].

1 *Macdonald* p 43.
2 *Gordon* para 16–17.

5.09 Piracy is not restricted to the actings of the crew of one ship against another ship. The crew of a ship can rise up and take masterful control of the ship from its lawful master, and that also constitutes piracy. Moreover, it is sufficient if there is only an attempt to take over control of a ship[1] and actual robbery is not essential to the crime[2].

1 Gordon para 16–17.
2 Gordon para 16–17, citing *Re Piracy jure gentium* [1934] AC 586.

5.10 The most modern (and most useful) definition of piracy is provided by Lord Cameron when he charged the jury in *Cameron v HM Advocate*[1]:

'if a ship on the high seas is unlawfully taken possession of by violence or by threat of violence, whether by persons from outside the ship or members of the crew, or passengers in the ship, and the ship is thereafter appropriated to the use of those who have seized it, that in law, if established, is the crime of piracy.'

1 1971 JC 50 at 56.

Tokyo Convention Act 1967

5.11 At common law, any person responsible for acts of piracy can be prosecuted in Scotland no matter where the acts of piracy were committed[1]. Thus piracy, as Hume stated[1], is an offence against the law of nations. However, as piracy is a crime of an international nature, Parliament enacted the Tokyo Convention Act 1967 with a view to ratification of the Convention on the High Seas signed at Geneva on 29 April 1958. It has been observed by the High Court in *Cameron* (supra) that the 1967 Act did not supersede, but was complementary to, the common law of Scotland.

1 *Hume* I, 480, although this fact apparently went unnoticed in the Appeal Court in *Cameron*; see Lord Justice-Clerk Wheatley's Opinion in *Cameron v HM Advocate* 1971 JC 50 at 60.

5.12 The 1967 Act is declaratory of the jurisdiction of the courts in the United Kingdom to try *inter alia*, piracy. The Act provides that any illegal acts of violence, detention or any act of depredation, committed for private ends by the crew or the passengers of a private ship and directed on the high seas against another ship, or against persons or property on board such ship, or against a ship, persons or property in a place outside the jurisdiction of any state, can be tried by the court of any state[1]. The Act also provides that these acts when committed by a warship whose crew has mutinied and taken control of the ship, are assimilated to acts committed by a private ship.

1 Tokyo Convention Act 1967, s 4 and Sch, art 15.

Hijacking

5.13 It would be a legal anachronism for the common law to have included within the definition of piracy, the forcible seizure of an aircraft. The Tokyo Convention Act 1967 accordingly makes the same provision for aircraft as it does for ships. However, the Aviation Security Act 1982 (which repealed the Hijacking Act 1971) provides that any person who, on board an aircraft which is in flight, by the use of force or by threats of any kind, seizes the aircraft or exercises control of it, commits the offence of hijacking. Hijacking is committed irrespective of the hijacker's nationality, the national registration of the aircraft or where the hijacking takes place[1]. It is also provided, however, that the offence is not committed if the aircraft is used in the military, customs or police service, or the places of take-off and landing are in the territory of the state in which the aircraft is registered, unless the accused is a United Kingdom national or his act is committed in the United Kingdom, or the aircraft is registered in the United Kingdom, or the aircraft is used in the service of the military or customs or a police authority in the United Kingdom[2]. The maximum penalty for hijacking is life imprisonment[3].

1 Tokyo Convention Act 1967, s 1(1).
2 Ibid, s 1(2).
3 Ibid, s 1(3).

6. Incest and related offences

6.01 Until the passing of the Incest and Related Offences (Scotland) Act 1986, the law regulating the crime of incest was contained in the Incest Act 1567. Incest was defined by Macdonald as carnal intercourse between near relations[1]. The carnal intercourse merely had to be the same as is prohibited by the law of rape. The 'near relations' were defined by the 1567 Act by reference to the eighteenth chapter of *Leviticus*, verses 6–18.

1 J H A Macdonald *The Criminal Law of Scotland* (5th edn, 1948) p 148; see G H Gordon *The Criminal Law of Scotland* (2nd edn, 1978) para 35–01.

6.02 The prohibited degrees of relationship were both very wide ranging and yet in some respects unnecessarily restricted. The law of incest, being derived from the sixteenth century when religious, social and moral opinions were different, was regarded as being inappropriate for modern times. For example, illegitimate relationships were excluded from the law of incest[1] with the one exception of a mother and her illegitimate son. Equally, though unsurprisingly, adoptive relationships were excluded from the law of incest. However, relationships which were constituted by affinity were included in the prohibited degrees although from a consideration of the importance of genetic health such prohibitions were unnecessary. Thus the Incest and Related Offences Act 1986 was passed thereby amending the Sexual Offences (Scotland) Act 1976 to make provision for a more restricted meaning of incest. The 1986 Act was based on recommendations of the Scottish Law Commission's report on the law of incest in Scotland[2].

1 Hume *Commentaries* I p 452; Alison *Principles* p 565; *Macdonald* p 148.
2 Law of Incest in Scotland (Scot Law Com no 69; Cmnd 8422 (23.12.81)).

6.03 Section 2A of the Sexual Offences (Scotland) Act 1976, by virtue of the amendment effected by the 1986 Act, provides that only certain consanguine and adoptive relationships constitute the crime of incest. Sexual intercourse between a male and his mother or daughter, grandmother or grand-daughter, sister, aunt, niece, great-grandmother or great-grand-daughter is incest; and *mutatis mutandis* the same relationships by consanguinity apply in respect of a female. Furthermore, a male who has sexual intercourse with his adoptive mother or former adoptive mother, or with his adoptive daughter or former adoptive daughter, is guilty of incest; and *mutatis mutandis* the same adoptive relationships apply in respect of a female. These relationships are prohibited relationships irrespective of whether they are full blood or half blood, or whether they are illegitimate[1].

1 Incest and Related Offences (Scotland) Act 1986, s 2A(2).

Statutory defences to incest

6.04 There are, however, defences provided under the 1976 Act for any person charged with incest. If the accused proves that he or she (a) did not know *and* had no reason to suspect that the person with whom he or she had sexual intercourse was related in one of the prohibited degrees; or (b) did not consent to have sexual intercourse or to have sexual intercourse with that person; or (c) was married to that person at the time when sexual intercourse took place by reason of a marriage contracted outside Scotland and recognised as valid by Scots law, then he or she is entitled to be acquitted of the crime of incest. It is thus clear that the new offence of incest is an offence of strict liability subject to the statutory defences being made out by the accused. It can no doubt be presumed in accordance with the general principles of Scots law that the defence will be made out if the accused establishes the facts under one or other of heads (a), (b), or (c) on balance of probability, and without the need for corroboration.

Sexual intercourse with a step-child

6.05 Section 2B of the Sexual Offences (Scotland) Act 1976 provides that any step-parent or former step-parent who has sexual intercourse with his or her step-child or former step-child is guilty of an offence if the step-child is either under 21 years of age or has at any time before attaining 18 years of age lived in the same household *and* been treated as a child of his or her family. This offence was created because of the removal from the law of incest of relationships by affinity as a recognition of the change in social and moral values which was not accommodated by the old law of incest[1].

1 Cf the Family Law (Scotland) Act 1985, s 1(1)(d).

Statutory defences

6.06 As in the case of the new offence of incest, the offence under s 2B of the 1976 Act is an offence of strict liability subject to the statutory defences that the accused shall not be guilty if he or she proves that he or she (a) did not know *and* had no reason to suspect that the person with whom he or she had sexual intercourse was a step-child or former step-child; or (b) believed on reasonable grounds that that person was of or over 21 years; or (c) did not consent to have sexual intercourse or to have sexual intercourse with that person; or (d) was married to that person at the time when sexual intercourse took place by reason of a marriage contracted outside Scotland and recognised as valid by Scots Law.

Abuse of trust

6.07 Certain children would not be protected by the new statutory offence of incest or by the provisions dealing with step-children and accordingly s 2C of the Sexual Offences (Scotland) Act 1976 provides that any person who is aged 16 years or over and who has sexual intercourse with a child under 16 years of age and is a member of the same household as that child, is guilty of an offence if he or she is in 'a position of trust or authority' in relation to that child. The phrase 'a position of trust or authority' is a question of fact and would depend upon the particular circumstances of each case. This offence also is an offence of strict liability subject only to three defences: if the accused proves that he or she (i) believed on reasonable grounds that the person with whom he or she had sexual intercourse was of or over the age of 16 years; or (ii) did not consent to have sexual intercourse or to have sexual intercourse with that person; or (iii) was married to that person at the time when the sexual intercourse took place by reason of a marriage contracted outside Scotland and recognised as valid by Scots law, then he or she will be entitled to acquittal.

The meaning of sexual intercourse

6.08 In both the case of incest under the Incest Act 1567 and the case of incest under s 2A of the Sexual Offences (Scotland) Act 1976, the crime is not committed unless sexual intercourse takes place. There is no good reason to consider that the meaning to be given to the use of the phrase 'sexual intercourse' should be any different under the 1976 Act than was the understanding of the prohibition contained in the 1567 Act. Since what constituted sexual intercourse for the purposes of the law of rape was also what amounted to sexual intercourse for incest under the 1567 Act[1], the same should hold for the new crime of incest. Equally, the offences under ss 2B and 2C should be treated in the same manner as the new offence of incest. Thus, of course, oral and anal intercourse are not included under any of the new offences.

1 See para 6.01, above.

Shamelessly indecent conduct

6.09 It has been held by the High Court that where a father committed sexual acts not amounting to sexual intercourse with his daughter who was 16 years of age at the time of the acts, the father was guilty of the crime of shameless indecency[1]. The High Court, under reference to the principles of the crime of shamelessly indecent conduct[2], held that since the time of Hume a sexual relationship between a parent and child has in the law of Scotland been regarded as behaviour which is repugnant to society[3].

1 *R v HM Advocate* 1988 SLT 623, 1988 SCCR 254.
2 See *Macdonald* p 150 and *Watt v Annan* 1978 SLT 198; 1978 JC 84.
3 *R v HM Advocate* 1988 SLT 623 at 625.

7. Physical offences involving indecency

7.01 This chapter is concerned with various common law and statutory offences which can involve an element of indecent physical contact between two people.

Sodomy

7.02 Historically, at common law the crime of sodomy is the unnatural carnal connection between male persons[1]. The crime is restricted to the following circumstances: it is committed by (a) anal penetration (b) of a male (c) by the penis of another. Both males are guilty of the crime if it is a consensual act. It is not sodomy to have anal intercourse with a woman although in certain circumstances it could amount to shamelessly indecent conduct. For example, a man who has anal intercourse with a woman in a public display in a 'sex show' would be liable to prosecution along with his partner for shameless indecency. Penetration of the anus to any extent is sufficient to constitute sodomy. Oral intercourse, whether with or without consent, is not sodomy although if the intercourse is obtained by force or threats of immediate physical harm, it is punishable as indecent assault.

1 Alison *Principles* p 566; J H A Macdonald p 149; G H Gordon *The Criminal Law of Scotland* (2nd edn, 1978) para 34–01.

7.03 Parliament to a limited extent 'de-criminalised' sodomy as a result of changes in public opinion. Section 80 of the Criminal Justice (Scotland) Act 1980 provides that a homosexual act (which includes sodomy) when committed in private shall not be an offence provided that the parties consent thereto and are 21 years of age or older. The 1980 Act however expressly excludes homosexual acts which are committed in a public lavatory or when more than two persons take part or are present, by providing that such acts are not to be treated as if they were done in private. The 1980 Act has no application to the armed forces. Thus it can be seen that the common law crime of sodomy is not abolished but merely restricted in its application.

7.04 Section 80(7) of the 1980 Act further creates the offence of committing or being a party to, or procuring or attempting to procure the commission of, a homosexual act (a) otherwise than in private; or (b) without the consent of both parties; or (c) with a person under 21 years of age; or (d) on board a United Kingdom registered merchant ship. It is, however, a defence to a charge under s 80(7)(c) (where the other party is under 21 years of age) for the accused to prove that he is under 24 years of age, has not previously been charged with a homosexual act and had reasonable cause to believe that the other person was 21 years of age or older[1].

1 Criminal Justice (Scotland) Act 1980, s 80(11).

Lewd, indecent and libidinous practices and behaviour

7.05 At common law it is a crime known by the phrase 'lewd, indecent and libidinous practices and behaviour' to use lewd practices towards children who are under the age of puberty[1]. Puberty in law is held to be 12 years of age for girls and 14 years for boys. It is irrelevant that the children consent to the practices. The lewd acts include, for example, indecent exposure in the presence of children or performing sexual acts in front of them; indecent handling of them; or inducing them to commit indecencies, and seducing and debauching them to these practices[2]. A woman may be convicted of using rude practices towards girls or boys[3].

1 *Macdonald* p 149; *Gordon* para 36–09.
2 *Macdonald* p 149.
3 *Gordon* para 36–09.

7.06 The essence of lewd, indecent and libidinous practices and behaviour is that the child victim is under the age of puberty[1]. The common law did not, however, protect girls aged 13 years or older and under 16 years of age. Thus s 5 of the Sexual Offences (Scotland) Act 1976 provides that it is an offence for any person to use any lewd, indecent or libidinous practice or behaviour which if used towards a girl under the age of 12 years would have constituted an offence at common law, and it is also provided that the girl's consent is irrelevant.

1 *Macdonald* p 150.

7.07 Section 3 of the Sexual Offences (Scotland) Act 1976 provides that it is an offence to have unlawful sexual intercourse with any girl under 13 years of age. It is an offence under s 4(1) of the 1976 Act to have or attempt to have unlawful sexual intercourse with a girl who is aged 13 years or above but under the age of 16 years. In both of these offences it is submitted that, since the offences are clearly designed to protect the girls, only the man can be guilty of the offence and the consent of the girl does not render her guilty of any offence by accession[1].

1 *Cf R v Tyrrell* [1894] 1 QB 710; *Gordon* para 5–05.

7.08 In respect of the offence under s 4(1), the 1976 Act does provide a statutory defence which is very similar to that provided for in the case of homosexual offences, under s 80(11) of the Criminal Justice (Scotland) Act 1980. It is a defence to a charge of unlawful sexual intercourse with a girl of or about 13 years of age and under 16 years of age that the accused is under 24 years of age, has not previously been charged with a like offence and had reasonable cause to believe that the girl was of or above the age of 16 years[1]. It is also provided[2] that it is a defence for the accused to show that he had reasonable cause to believe that the girl was his wife.

1 Sexual Offences (Scotland) Act 1976, s 4(2)(b).
2 Ibid, s 4(2)(a).

8. Self defence

Self defence and homicide

8.01 This chapter is concerned with the special defence of self defence. The law regulating the availability of the defence has been developed principally in connection with cases of criminal homicide and accordingly this chapter will deal only with the law relating to self defence as a defence to a charge of murder or culpable homicide. The defence is of course available to persons accused of assault but the rules relating to self defence are as a matter of judicial practice applied less strictly in such cases.

Private defence

8.02 The term 'self defence' is misleading because it implies that only a person who is himself the victim of an attack, is entitled to defend himself. The defence is, however, available where A kills B in order to protect the life of C who is being attacked by B[1]. The more accurate description of the defence is therefore 'private defence' but since this expression is rarely, if ever, used in Scotland, the term self defence will be employed in this chapter.

1 Hume *Commentaries* I, 218; J H A Macdonald *The Criminal Law of Scotland* (5th edn, 1948) p 106; *HM Advocate v Carson* 1964 SLT 21.

Effect of self defence

8.03 The effect of a successful plea of self defence is that the accused is acquitted. The basis of the acquittal is that the homicide which was admittedly committed, was justified by the violent attack of the deceased. Exculpation is always the sole function of the special defence of self defence[1]. The successful defence negatives the *mens rea* of murder because the accused's intention is not to commit a criminal assault on the victim but to prevent the victim from carrying out an assault on another person³. Accordingly if an accused person advances a plea of self defence the burden of proof remains with the Crown throughout to prove the crime charged. The mere fact that the accused advances a plea of self defence by implication admits the performance of the act or some of the acts with which the accused is charged but it does not in any way lessen the burden of proof on the Crown because that implied admission has got to be taken with its qualification, namely that these acts were done in self defence and are therefore not of a criminal quality³.

1 *Crawford v HM Advocate* 1950 JC 67.
2 *HM Advocate v Carson* 1964 SLT 21.
3 *HM Advocate v Brogan* 1964 SLT 204.

Provocation and self defence distinguished

8.04 Since the time of Hume there has been considerable confusion in Scots law over the distinction between the defence of self defence and the defence of provocation. The confusion, it is here suggested, arose from the distinction which Hume drew between (1) self defence in cases where there was an unprovoked attack on an entirely innocent person, and (2) self defence advanced by someone who was involved in a quarrel[1]. In the former case Hume considered that the victim of the unprovoked assault was entitled to

'secure himself by the only certain means, the immediate death of the assailant; who is no true man, to be contended with on equal terms, but a foul criminal... and the fit object, therefore, of extreme and summary justice[2]'.

In the latter case the victim had to use only minimum force for his own safety. No such distinction is now recognised in Scots law which requires in all cases that only reasonable force be used. However, this unnecessary (and now incorrect) distinction obscured Hume's recognition elsewhere of the difference between murder and 'homicide on provocation[3]' where provocation only mitigated sentence, such that Macdonald when dealing with assault, could state in 1945 that provocation by blows 'will justify retaliation in self defence if not excessive[4]'. This view was erroneous because there is no logical difference between assault and murder such that provocation can result in acquittal in some cases of assault. The same confusion indeed was evident in 1965[5]. However, the error established in Hume, was extended to murder. Thus in *HM Advocate v Kizileviczius*[6], Lord Jamieson directed the jury that if they found that the accused had used excessive self defence they could return a verdict of guilty of culpable homicide⁷.

1 See *Hume* I, 217.
2 *Hume* I, 218.
3 *Hume* I, 246.
4 *Macdonald* p 116.
5 See R J D Scott 'The Doctrine of Provocation' 1965 SLT (News) 193.
6 1938 JC 60.
7 See also *Hillan v HM Advocate* 1937 JC 53 at 57, per Lord Justice-Clerk Aitchison.

Excessive self defence

8.05 The erroneous conflation of provocation and self defence was ended by the Appeal Court in *Crawford v HM Advocate*¹, where the distinction between self defence and provocation was finally established. Self defence results in acquittal, but provocation only reduces a crime of murder to culpable homicide, or otherwise mitigates the sentence. Thus both *HM Advocate v Kizileviczius*², and *Hillan v HM Advocate*³, wrongly state the law. Thus it is also clear that Scots law does not recognise the defence of excessive self defence, or unjustifiable self defence, which reduces murder to culpable homicide⁴. This is made clear in *Fenning v HM Advocate*⁵, where the accused appealed against conviction on the ground inter alia that the trial judge had wrongly failed to direct the jury that even if they were not satisfied that the accused had acted in self defence, they could nevertheless find him guilty of culpable homicide if they considered that while in a state of danger, the accused, without any intention to kill, had used unnecessary violence or had continued to use violence after the danger had passed. The accused in effect was seeking a direction as was given in *Kizileviczius* but on the authority of *Crawford*, the Appeal Court rejected that ground of appeal. Excessive use of force loses the accused the right to found on self defence. In these circumstances if the accused is to avoid conviction for murder he must establish provocation.

1 1950 JC 67.
2 1938 JC 60.
3 1937 JC 53.
4 See *Gordon* para 25–17.
5 1985 SCCR 219, 1985 SLT 540.

8.06 The logic of *Crawford* requires therefore that when an accused pleads both self defence and provocation, the jury must approach each plea separately. The solution to the issues raised by these pleas is dependent upon quite distinct and distinguishable factual circumstances, and these pleas are not matters of concurrent consideration[1]. The jury must first consider whether the accused acted in self defence, and only once that plea is rejected should they then consider the question of provocation.

1 *Fenning v HM Advocate* 1985 SCCR 219 at 225, 1985 SLT 540 at 544, per Lord Cameron.

The requirements of self defence

8.07 For an accused to be entitled to acquittal on the ground of self defence a jury must be satisfied that four conditions are met. These were set out by Lord Keith in the case of *HM Advocate v Doherty*[1], and are consistently given to juries in cases where self defence is raised.

1 1954 JC 1.

The nature of the danger

8.08 First, the accused must have been faced with danger to his life. A danger of minor assault or of an assault which would clearly not amount to a fatal assault, will not suffice. In *Doherty* Lord Keith referred to danger to 'life or limb', but that reference must be taken to imply only that the threat must be of at least serious bodily harm such that an accused would be unable to determine at the time whether the danger did not involve the threat of death. What is essential is that life is endangered. Being 'gravely threatened' by a man with a knife can be sufficient to satisfy this condition[1]. As Lord Justice-General Clyde said in *McCluskey v HM Advocate*[2]:

'Our law has always held that if there are reasonable grounds for a person apprehending that his life is in danger he is entitled to protect himself'.

1 *Owens v HM Advocate* 1946 JC 119 at 125.
2 1959 JC 39.

Imminent danger

8.09 Secondly, if the accused is threatened with danger to life in the future, the accused has no right to use fatal force because he is then acting prematurely, and therefore unjustifiably. He thereby loses his right to acquittal on the ground of self defence. The danger must therefore be imminent or immediate[1]. It follows that a pre-emptive strike can never amount to self defence in Scots law although this is not the case in English law[2].

1 Alison *Principles* p 132. See eg Lord Dunpark's charge in *Jones v HM Advocate* 1989 SCCR 726 at 730.
2 Cf *Beckford v R* [1987] 3 All ER 425.

No means of escape

8.10 Thirdly, for self defence to be available there must be no reasonable means of escape[1]:

'if the person assaulted has means of escape or retreat, he is bound to use them. If he has these means, then it is not necessary in self defence to stand up against the other man[2]'.

This rule is seen as particularly severe and is not now applied in England[3] where the presence of means of escape is only a factor to be taken into account in considering the reasonableness of the accused's whole conduct.

1 *Hume* I, 226; *Macdonald* p 106.
2 *HM Advocate v Doherty* 1954 JC 1.
3 *R v Bird* [1985] 2 All ER 513.

The retaliation must be reasonable

8.11 Fourthly, the accused must use no more than reasonable force in defence of himself or another person. He is not entitled to go beyond what is necessary for his own safety[1]. The degree of force which is in law permissible to repel an attack must be adjusted to the violence and quality of the attack which has to be repelled[2]. The defence of self defence is not a licence to use force grossly in excess of that necessary to defend oneself[3]. Cruel excess loses the accused the right to self defence. It is, however, the practice for juries to be told in addition that they should not weigh the retaliation in too fine scales, that they should make allowance for the heat of blood and excitement at the time of the attack. As Hume stated, the judge will not insist on an exact proportion of injury and retaliation but rather will be disposed to sustain the defence 'unless the pannel has been transported to acts of cruelty or great excess' because allowance must be given for the fact that there is no time for reflection[4]. However, use of phrases such as 'heat of blood', and 'allowance for excitement', etc, are not mandatory; if the jury are directed that there must be no cruel excess, that will be sufficient without recourse to ritualistic phrases[5].

1 *HM Advocate v Doherty* 1954 JC 1.
2 *Fenning v HM Advocate* 1985 SCCR 219, 1985 SLT 540.
3 *Hume* I, 228, 229.
4 *Hume* I, 335. See *Hillan v HM Advocate* 1937 JC 53 at 64, per Lord Wark; *Moore v MacDougall* 1989 SCCR 659.
5 *Fenning v HM Advocate* 1985 SCCR 219, 1985 SLT 540.

Self defence against rape

8.12 The institutional writers[1] accepted that a woman was entitled to kill in defence of her chastity; and therefore anyone is entitled to kill a rapist if this is necessary to prevent rape[2]. This is the one extension of the defence of self defence which Scots law recognises. It is an exception to the rule that homicide is only justifiable when the homicide is committed to save life. Moreover such an exception to the general rule also presumably justifies A in killing not only B, who is attempting to commit rape on D, but also C, a woman who is assisting B, where it is necessary to do so.

1 *Hume* I, 218; Alison *Principles* p 132.
2 *Macdonald* p 107.

8.13 The question therefore arises whether a man is entitled to kill in order to prevent an act of forcible sodomy being committed against him. In *McCluskey v HM Advocate*[1] the Appeal Court rejected such a view which it regarded as an extension of the doctrine of self defence for which there was no authority and for which, according to Lord Justice-General Clyde, there was no logical or indeed any other justification. The Appeal Court refuted the suggested parallel which was drawn between rape and sodomy on the basis that rape 'involves complete absence of consent on the part of the woman'. This distinction must, however, be unsound since forcible sodomy as was in issue in *McCluskey*, necessarily involves the absence of consent on the part of the accused. However, the principal ground of decision in *McCluskey* was stated by Lord Justice-General Clyde in the following terms:

'Where an attack by an accused person on another man has taken place and where the object of the attack has been to ward off an assault upon him it is essential that the attack should be made to save the accused's life before the plea of self defence can succeed. For myself, I would be slow indeed to suggest that people in this country are justified in taking life merely because their honour is assailed by someone else[2].

The decision in *McCluskey* was followed in *Elliott v HM Advocate*[3] which must give room for doubting the propriety of the exception in favour of people who kill to prevent rape.

1 1959 JC 39.
2 1959 JC 39 at 43.
3 1987 SCCR 278.

Is homicide justifiable in defence of property?

8.14 Hume stated that there could be cases where it would be justifiable to kill although there was no imminent danger to life[1]. Hume considered the possibility of A the owner of a horse, in some remote place finding B stealing his horse and failing to stop when called on to do so by A, and concluded that there seemed to be no sound law which should hinder A from saving his property though it involved killing B. Burnett[2] followed Hume's view but Alison[3] dissented on the utilitarian view that the law could not permit an individual citizen to inflict a more severe pain with his own hand than it would impose if the thief were convicted for the offence in a court of law[4]. It is personal danger, not patrimonial loss, which justifies homicide[5].

1 *Hume* I, 222.
2 Burnett *The Criminal Law of Scotland* (1811), p 57.
3 Alison *Principles* pp 22–23.
4 See *Jas Craw* (1826) Syme 188 at 210, and *Kennedy* (1829). See also Alison *Principles* p 23; *Gordon* para 24–04.
5 *Macdonald* p 107.

Homicide in mistaken belief of attack

8.15 If A kills in the mistaken belief that B is attacking him (or a third party), A is entitled to plead self defence only if the mistaken belief was based on reasonable grounds[1]. The defence is available to an accused to ward off danger 'which was actually threatened or danger which might reasonably be anticipated' by the accused[2]. If the accused did not reasonably apprehend danger to himself or another, he is not entitled to plead self defence. There must be an objective justification for the accused's belief that he is being attacked[3].

1 *Owens v HM Advocate* 1946 JC 119; followed in *Jones v HM Advocate* 1989 SCCR 726.
2 *McCluskey v HM Advocate* 1959 JC 39 at 40, per Lord Strachan.
3 *Crawford v HM Advocate* 1950 JC 67.

8.16 The rule that unreasonable error will not justify acting in self defence may appear to be somewhat severe[1]. It is, however, applied by the courts in order to minimise the risk of juries being gullible enough to believe outrageous assertions of error made by accused persons. But the requirement is inconsistent with the development in the law of rape where it has been held that an accused is not guilty of rape if he genuinely believed that his victim was consenting even if his belief was unreasonable[2]. The only importance of the belief being unreasonable in rape is that it can cast doubt on the credibility of the accused when he maintains that he believed that she consented. It has been recognised in England that the principle in *Meek v HM Advocate*[2], extends beyond the law of rape[3]. Thus, the Privy Council has held in an appeal from Jamaica (though applicable generally in English law) that if a plea of self defence is raised in a trial for murder when the accused has acted under a mistake of fact, he is to be judged according to his mistaken belief regardless of whether, viewed objectively, his mistake was reasonable[4].

1 See generally *Gordon* paras 9–16 to 9–32.
2 *Meek v HM Advocate* 1982 SCCR 613, 1983 SLT 280.
3 Smith and Hogan *Criminal Law* (6th edn) p 86.
4 *Beckford v R* [1987] 3 All ER 425 at 432 per Lord Griffiths; see also *R v Williams* [1987] 3 All ER 411.

Accident and self defence

8.17 The law recognises that death can be caused by accident on the part of an accused who is accordingly not guilty of homicide[1]. The difficulty arises in certain trials for murder where the accused pleads self defence, provocation and accident[2]. What is the relationship between accident and self defence? It has been said in the Appeal Court that an accused is always entitled to have the jury consider a defence based on accidental homicide[3]. It remains, however, a question for the trial judge whether there is sufficient evidence for the jury to be required to consider the issue of self defence. An accused is not automatically entitled to have self defence go to the jury although it is always a strong step for a trial judge to withdraw a special defence from the jury's consideration[4].

1 See *HM Advocate v Rutherford* 1947 JC 1.
2 Eg *Graham v HM Advocate* 1987 SCCR 20.
3 *MacKenzie v HM Advocate* 1983 SLT 220 at 224, per Lord Avonside.
4 *Crawford v HM Advocate* 1950 JC 67; *Kennedy v HM Advocate* 1950 JC 67.

8.18 If accident and self defence are both pled, it may be wrong for the trial judge to withdraw the defence of accident on the reasoning that self defence and accident are mutually exclusive, because there are circumstances where that is not so[1]. In *MacKenzie v HM Advocate*[2], the accused took out a knife and threatened the deceased with it in order to defend himself, and thereafter in the course of a struggle, the deceased was fatally stabbed. The trial judge withdrew the issue of accident, and the Appeal Court held that to be a misdirection. The error in *MacKenzie* was for the trial judge to hold the defences to be mutually inconsistent when in fact there was no real issue of self defence at all since the substantial defence was that death was caused by the deceased's accidentally impaling himself when he lunged forward at the accused. It all depends upon the particular circumstances whether in each individual case the defence of accident excludes the possibility of the accused having acted in self defence[3].

1 *HM Advocate v Woods* 1972 SLT (Notes) 77.
2 1983 SLT 220.
3 *Surman v HM Advocate* 1988 SLT 371.

9. Provocation

9.01 Scots law recognises provocation as a distinct defence to a charge of murder. Provocation is, of course, also available as a plea in mitigation in charges of assault but its most important use is as a defence to a charge of murder where, if successful, its effect is to reduce the crime from murder to culpable homicide[1]. Provocation is a plea in mitigation of intentional killing[2], and is thus a specific defence to murder. It is provocation of that sort which is considered in this chapter.

1 *Brady v HM Advocate* 1986 SLT 686 at 688.
2 G H Gordon *The Criminal Law of Scotland* (2nd edn, 1978) para 25-09.

Provocation and self defence

9.02 Since provocation is concerned with the partial justification or excusal of an accused's homicidal actings, it has always been and still is rarely pled by an accused other than in tandem with a defence of self defence[1]. However, the pleas of provocation and self defence should not be confused. As Lord Justice-General Clyde said in *Crawford v HM Advocate*[2], while the facts relied upon to support a plea of self defence usually contain 'a strong element of provocation', the pleas are not identical but are entirely separate and distinct[3].

1 See ch 8, above.
2 *Crawford v HM Advocate* 1950 SLT 279 at 281, per Lord Justice-General Clyde.
3 See also *HM Advocate v Kizileviczius* 1938 SLT 245, per Lord Jamieson; *Hillan v HM Advocate* 1937 SLT 396 at 397, per Lord Justice-Clerk Aitchison; and *Fenning v HM Advocate* 1985 SCCR 219 at 225, 1985 SLT 540 at 544, per Lord Cameron.

The requirements of provocation

9.03 The plea of provocation can only succeed where certain requirements are satisfied. The classic description of provocation is provided by Macdonald:

'Being agitated and excited, and alarmed by violence, I lost control over myself and took life, when my presence of mind had left me, and without thought of what I was doing¹'.

These words were adopted by Lord Jamieson in his charge to the jury in *HM Advocate v Kizilevicius*², and have remained the law ever since. The essence of provocation is that the accused must have lost control over himself. Macdonald's description does not, however, state the defence of provocation in its entirety because certain restrictions are imposed on the applicability of provocation as described by Macdonald.

1 J H A Macdonald *The Criminal Law of Scotland* (5th edn, 1948) p 94.
2 1938 SLT 245.

There must be an assault

9.04 The first requirement is that, with one exception, in order for an accused to found a defence of provocation there must have been a serious assault committed by the person whom the accused kills[1]. The assault must not be minor but must be a substantial assault. Sheriff Gordon[2] suggests that assault although of a minor nature is probably now sufficient to constitute provocation. There is, however, no authority for this view and there is now clear authority against it[3]. Accordingly, Scots law does not recognise provocation by insults or threats although there have been certain cases which have suggested that verbal provocation can succeed even though there has been no physical assault[4]. These cases must now be considered to be wrong in the light of the opinions delivered in *Thomson v HM Advocate*[5].

1 Hume *Commentaries* I, 247–248; Alison *Principles* p 21; *Macdonald* p 93.
2 *Gordon* para 25–25.
3 *Thomson v HM Advocate* 1985 SCCR 448. See also *Cosgrove v HM Advocate* (28 March 1990, unreported), Court of Criminal Appeal.
4 Eg *Stobbs v HM Advocate* 1983 SCCR 190; *Berry v HM Advocate* 1976 SCCR Supp 156.
5 1985 SCCR 448. See PWF 'The Doctrine of Provocation' 1986 SLT (News) 171.

9.05 In *Thomson* the accused was convicted of murdering his former business associate by stabbing him eleven times with a knife on the legs, arms and body. The accused pled provocation on the basis that the deceased had cheated the accused over a period of time and when eventually the accused confronted the deceased, the deceased laughed at him and physically restrained him. The trial judge withdrew provocation from the jury's consideration. The Appeal Court refused the appeal against conviction which was taken on the basis that the trial judge had misdirected the jury in withdrawing provocation from their consideration. Whether looked at individually or together, the evidence of the business dealings and the minor assault were held by the Appeal Court to be insufficient to entitle the jury to consider provocation. Lord Justice-Clerk Ross explained that minor assault was insufficient to palliate killing because there must be some relation between the force used against the accused and the violence of the retaliation.

Adultery cases

9.06 The one exception which Scots law admits to the rule excluding provocation except in cases of serious assault, is where the accused has killed when discovering his or her spouse's adultery. Originally, the exception was applied only to the discovery of the spouse in the act of adultery[1], but it has been successively extended by the courts to include a confession of adultery[2] and the discovery of a wife in bed with her lesbian paramour[3]. In *McDermott v HM Advocate*[4], Lord Cameron allowed provocation to go to the jury where the illicit association was between the victim and the accused's girlfriend. The adultery cases can be distinguished from cases in which verbal provocation has been present because the adultery cases do not involve insulting or threatening remarks but a statement of fact which causes the accused temporarily to lose his self control[5]. However, the distinction is not strong and implicitly recognises that certain actions not amounting to serious assault can nonetheless cause a person to lose his self control.

1 *Hume* I, 245; *Gordon* para 25–24.
2 *HM Advocate v Hill* 1941 JC 59.
3 *HM Advocate v Callander* 1958 SLT 24.
4 1976 JC 8.
5 See *Gordon* para 25–24.

Delay excludes provocation

9.07 The second requirement for provocation to be successfully pled is that the assault must immediately precede the killing[1]. In *Thomson v HM Advocate*[2], Lord-Justice Clerk Ross considered that since the accused had acted under the influence of what he had known for several days, there could be no provocation. The provocation must be such as to overcome the accused's self control at the time of the killing and delay contradicts the essence of provocation. The requirement that there be no interval between the provocative act and the retaliation applies also in the adultery cases[3].

1 *Macdonald* p 94; *HM Advocate v Callander* 1958 SLT 24.
2 1985 SCCR 448.
3 *HM Advocate v Hill* 1941 JC 59.

Cumulative provocation

9.08 Cumulative provocation is a prolonged course of conduct which gradually induces the accused to lose his self control but in which there is no ultimate serious assault committed by the deceased immediately preceding the killing. In *HM Advocate v Greig*[1], there was evidence that the accused's husband was a drunkard, a bully, and that he had assaulted the accused from time to time making her life misery. Lord Dunpark allowed provocation to go to the jury but observed that he could not find any evidence that the accused had been provoked. In *Crawford v HM Advocate*[2], Lord Mackay left the issue of provocation to the jury where there was evidence of domestic unhappiness but no serious assault, in respect of an accused who killed his father after frequently quarrelling with him. Both these cases were disapproved in *Thomson v HM Advocate*[3], which also is authority for the view that cumulative provocation is not recognised by Scots law. Cumulative provocation is rejected because it suggests the opposite of a sudden loss of self control. Rather than suggesting provocation, it is, as Lord Hunter said in *Thomson*, suggestive of motive[4]. However, although it is the final assault which must be committed when self control is lost, it is nonetheless relevant to consider the whole conduct of the deceased prior to his death notwithstanding the fact that this approach was not accepted by the Appeal Court in *Graham v HM Advocate*[5].

1 (May 1979, unreported), High Court of Justiciary.
2 1950 JC 67.
3 1985 SCCR 448.
4 See *Macdonald* p 94.
5 1987 SCCR 20.

There must not be 'cruel excess'

9.09 The third restriction on provocation is that the retaliation must not be excessive. Where the victim has used force there must be some relation between that force and the violence of the retaliation[1]. As Lord Justice-General Cooper directed the jury in *HM Advocate v Smith*[2]:

'A blow with the fist is no justification for the use of a lethal weapon. Provocation, in short, must bear a reasonable retaliation to the resentment which it excites'.

To a large extent, however, this requirement is unnecessary because the law does not recognise provocation other than by serious assault. It is, accordingly, difficult to understand the need for a reasonableness test when it is also accepted that the degree of retaliation should not be measured in too fine scales.

1 *Thomson v HM Advocate* 1985 SCCR 448.
2 (February 1952, unreported), High Court of Justiciary.

Indirect provocation

9.10 Although there is no modern judicial authority on the question, it may be that A may be entitled to plead provocation by B if B seriously assaults C. Hume records the case of *McGhie*[1], in which the accused founded on 'the provocation and alarm of a violent assault, made by the man on his father in his presence'. The relevance of this kind of indirect provocation can be justifed by analogy with the same rule that A may kill B in order to save C's life[2].

1 (1791): See *Hume* I, 246.
2 *HM Advocate v Carson* 1964 SLT 21; *Gordon* para 25–21.

Reasonable error and provocation

9.11 Just as it is accepted that A may kill while labouring under a reasonable error as to the necessity of acting in self defence[1], it is now also recognised that a reasonable error can be the basis for pleading provocation[2]. The belief must not, however, be an unreasonable belief. If it is an unreasonable belief the accused loses the defence of provocation.

1 *Owens v HM Advocate* 1946 JC 119.
2 *Jones v HM Advocate* 1989 SCCR 726.

Attempted murder

9.12 Although there is no mandatory sentence of life imprisonment which must be imposed in the event of a conviction for attempted murder, the Appeal Court has held that the effect of a successful plea of provocation in a case of attempted murder is to reduce the crime to assault under provocation. In *Brady v HM Advocate*[1], the Appeal Court quashed a conviction for attempted murder under provocation as incompetent because the *mens rea* of attempted murder is held to be the same as that for murder[2]. Lord Justice-Clerk Ross explained in *Brady*:

'If the charge is murder and the accused is successful in a plea of provocation the offence is reduced to culpable homicide. There is no question of such an accused being found guilty of murder under provocation upon the view that the killing under provocation is not deliberate or the result of wicked recklessness. If that is so I am of opinion that, when the charge is one of attempted murder, if the plea of provocation succeeds there can be no question of a verdict being returned of attempted murder under provocation'.

The decision in *Brady* is, however, at odds with Alison's view[3] where he suggests that the appropriate verdict is attempted culpable homicide. The Scottish Law Commission has also argued that it may be reasonable to allow provocation to lead to such a verdict[4].

1 1986 SLT 686.
2 *Cawthorne v HM Advocate* 1968 JC 32.
3 Alison *Principles* p 165.
4 Consultative Memorandum on Attempted Homicide no 61 (1984), para 5.3.

10. Diminished responsibility

Murder and diminished responsibility

10.01 The plea of diminished responsibility, like the plea of provocation, is strictly speaking limited to the crime of murder. The effect of a successful defence of diminished responsibility is not acquittal but reduction of the crime from murder to culpable homicide. Its effect is on the nature and quality of the crime[1] such that sentence ought to be mitigated[2]. Diminished responsibility as a concept originated in the times of capital punishment and was intended to allow an accused person to avoid being hanged without having to comply with the strict requirements of the defence of insanity. As a plea in mitigation, however, diminished responsibility is a relevant plea for all criminal charges despite statements to the contrary in both *HM Advocate v Cunningham*[3] and *Brennan v HM Advocate*[4].

1 See *HM Advocate v Blake* 1986 SLT 661.
2 Cf G H Gordon *The Criminal Law of Scotland* (2nd edn, 1978) para 11–04.
3 1963 JC 80, 1963 SLT 345.
4 1977 SLT 151.

Definition of diminished responsibility

10.02 The defence of diminished responsibility is recognised by the courts in Scotland as being properly defined by what Lord Justice-Clerk Alness told the jury in *HM Advocate v Savage*[1]:

'... there must be aberration or weakness of mind; that there must be some form of mental unsoundness; that there must be a state of mind which is bordering on, though not amounting to, insanity; that there must be a mind so affected that responsibility is diminished from full responsibility to partial responsibility—in other words, the prisoner in question must be only partially accountable for his actions.'

Lord Justice-Clerk Alness added that there must be some form of 'mental disease'. The direction in *Savage* was approved by a Full

Bench of five Judges of the High Court in *Carraher v HM Advocate*[2] and was the basis of a direction to the jury on diminished responsibility in *HM Advocate v Braithwaite*[3]. The direction in *Savage* is now regarded as the *locus classicus* on the subject of diminished responsibility[4].

1 1923 JC 49 at 51.
2 1946 JC 108.
3 1945 JC 55.
4 *Gordon* para 11–19. See *Connelly v HM Advocate* (5 June 1990, unreported), Court of Criminal Appeal, where the four criteria of diminished responsibility referred to by Lord Justice-Clerk Alness in *HM Advocate v Savage* 1923 JC 49 were held to be read as cumulative and not as alternatives.

Psychopathic personality

10.03 The defence of diminished responsibility is not capable of being extended beyond its scope as defined in *Savage*. There must be something approaching insanity, or mental disease, an aberration of the mind or great peculiarity such as to impair the accused's responsibility for his actions. In *Carraher* the accused was convicted of murder by stabbing. There was evidence that the accused suffered from a psychopathic personality and that he had consumed a considerable amount of drink before the fatal assault. The medical evidence described the psychopathic person as being someone who has difficulty in resisting temptation and could not withstand frustration; psychopaths were people who exhibited a gross abnormality in their social behaviour and emotional reaction but who did not as a rule show enough insanity to be certifiable. The trial judge allowed diminished responsibility to go to the jury. The Appeal Court entertained great doubt as to whether the medical evidence was evidence of anything approaching to mental disease, aberration or great peculiarity of mind and wondered whether the trial judge might not have been warranted in withdrawing diminished responsibility from the jury. Despite the hesitation expressed elsewhere[1], *Carraher* is clear authority for two propositions, namely: (a) the plea of diminished responsibility should not be extended or given wider scope than it has hitherto been accorded in previous decisions[2]; (b) psychopaths in particular are not entitled to found on a plea of diminished responsibility.

1 *Gordon* para 11–21.
2 *Carraher v HM Advocate* 1946 JC 108 at 118.

10.04 The decision in *Carraher* is readily understandable in the light of the medical evidence in that case. As Lord Justice-General Normand said:

'The court has a duty to see that trial by judge and jury according to law is not subordinated to medical theories[1]; and in this instance much of the evidence given by the medical witnesses is, to my mind, descriptive rather of a typical criminal than of a person with the quality of one whom the law has hitherto regarded as being possessed of diminished responsibility'[2].

Carraher is, however, only an example of the restrictive interpretation which is placed on the defence of diminished responsibility. The central feature of diminished responsibility is that there must be a real mental infirmity or impairment. Any slight departure from the normal make-up of a man will not do[3]. Thus an eccentricity of character or oddity of nature will not suffice. There must be some medical psychiatric evidence which justifies concluding that the accused's responsibility for his actions was below normal. For example, a person who regularly commits serious violent and unprovoked crime might be regarded as suffering from diminished responsibility but as was observed in *Carraher*, he may in truth simply be a criminal. In *HM Advocate v Blake*[3] the accused went into a medical centre and while in the surgery, struck his victim on the head, arms and hands with an axe. Lord Brand in directing the jury on diminished responsibility drew the jury's attention to a distinction between something in the nature of a mental disease and a vicious tendency, between 'the mentally sick and the morally bad'.

1 This statement was approved by Lord Justice-General Hope in *Connelly v HM Advocate* (5 June 1990, unreported), Court of Criminal Appeal.
2 1946 JC 108 at 117.
3 *HM Advocate v Blake* 1986 SLT 661.

The retreat from Carraher

10.05 The decision in *Carraher* is of course binding on trial judges who would thereby not be permitted to allow juries to consider diminished responsibility where the only evidence amounted to proof of psychopathic personality. *Carraher* has consequently been ignored in practice by the Crown when it has seemed appropriate to do so. The Crown can accept a plea of guilty to culpable homicide on the grounds of the accused's diminished responsibility even where he is a psychopath so long as the State hospital is prepared to make a bed available. The court is then enabled to make a hospital order under s 175 of the Criminal Procedure (Scotland) Act 1975 detaining the accused in a hospital. In these circumstances the court can indeed specify that the accused should be detained in the State hospital at Carstairs on account of his dangerous, violent or criminal propensities which require treatment under conditions of special security, and because he cannot suitably be cared for in a hospital other than a State hospital[1]. It is, however, worthy of note that psychiatric medicine is not yet a uniform body of knowledge since in at least one case (*Allan v HM Advocate*[2]) the psychiatric evidence was conflicting over whether the accused's psychopathic personality could constitute a mental disorder so as to qualify the accused for a mental health disposal under s 175 of the Criminal Procedure (Scotland) Act 1975. With that sort of confusion it is little wonder that the High Court decided *Carraher* as it did; and still less cause for wonder that *Carraher* has never been reconsidered.

1 See the Criminal Procedure (Scotland) Act 1975, s 175(4).
2 1983 SCCR 183.

Onus on the accused

10.06 As in the defence of insanity, the onus rests on the accused to establish that at the material time he was suffering from diminished responsibility. The accused is presumed to be of good mental health until the contrary is established. The standard of proof is, however, relaxed in favour of the accused who need only satisfy the civil standard of balance of probability[1].

1 *HM Advocate v Blake* 1986 SLT 661.

Diminished responsibility and other crimes

10.07 The plea of diminished responsibility is theoretically regarded as being limited to murder because it reduces the crime of murder to culpable homicide. In these circumstances diminished responsibility affects the character of the offence in cases of homicide. Thus it has perhaps been considered to be inappropriate to refer to diminished responsibility in the non-murder cases. However, as the late Professor T B Smith submitted, the true value of diminished responsibility is that its primary purpose is to mitigate punishment generally[1]. Thus although the name or character of the offence is not necessarily affected, a rapist or wilful fire-raiser for example, can also avail himself of the plea. Indeed, Lord Brand in *HM Advocate v Blake*[2] directed the jury that if diminished responsibility were established by the accused who was charged with attempted murder, the appropriate verdict would be assault[3]. Moreover, Macdonald[4] stated that, in principle, diminished responsibility could operate in cases of assault, and Lord Keith in an article published in 1959 considered that diminished responsibility could as a matter of principle operate outside cases of homicide[5]. In *Miller v HM Advocate*[6], for example, the Appeal Court reduced a sentence in respect of firearms offences and breach of the peace on account of the fact that the Crown accepted that the accused suffered from a disorientated and disturbed mental condition at the time of the offences.

1 See T B Smith *A Short Commentary on the Law of Scotland* (1962) p 153.
2 1986 SLT 661.
3 Cf *Brady v HM Advocate* 1986 SLT 686 where a similar view was taken in cases of provocation.
4 J H A Macdonald *The Criminal Law of Scotland* (5th edn, 1948) p 117.
5 'Some observations on diminished responsibility' 1959 JR 109 at 113.
6 1987 GWD 7–216.

Sentencing

10.08 The matter is, however, largely academic because, apart from murder cases, the sentence to be imposed is a question of discretion for the trial judge. The effect of diminished responsibility in murder cases is, as Sheriff Gordon expresses it, only a device to avoid the mandatory penalty of life imprisonment for murder prescribed by s 205(1) of the Criminal Procedure (Scotland) Act 1975[1]. If the accused is convicted of murder, then he cannot be dealt with under the provisions of s 175 of the 1975 Act because the sentence is fixed by law. In all other cases the court can make an order if it is appropriate in the circumstances. Equally, of course, the court is only entitled to make a hospital order when it is satisfied that the accused is suffering from a mental disorder of such a degree which makes it appropriate for him to receive medical treatment in a hospital[2]. Thus, if the Crown were to accept a plea to culpable homicide on the basis of diminished responsibility and the psychiatric evidence were not to satisfy the court because it was conflicting, the accused could simply be sentenced as an ordinary offender. In a case of attempted rape (*Allan v HM Advocate*[3]), where there was of course no question of the Crown accepting a 'reduced plea', the evidence was conflicting on whether the accused suffered from a mental disorder and in view of the high risk of repetition of assault on women and boys by the accused, the trial judge sentenced the accused to life imprisonment. The Appeal Court refused the appeal against sentence on the ground that the sentence being indeterminate was the most humane disposal available. The Appeal Court in *Donaldson v HM Advocate*[4] (following *Allan*) also upheld a sentence of life imprisonment imposed on a

19-year-old girl in respect of charges of wilful fire-raising. The accused was described as showing evidence of a most severe form of psychopathic personality with sadistic and aggressive features, and she was said to be likely to remain highly dangerous for many years to come. Both *Allan* and *Donaldson* also indicated that psychopathy when it is the eventual diagnosis, is a condition which is better dealt with by imprisonment than confinement in a hospital as *Carraher* recognised many years ago[5].

1 *Gordon* para 11–04.
2 See the Mental Health (Scotland) Act 1984, s 17(1)(a)(i).
3 *Allan v HM Advocate* 1983 SCCR 183.
4 1983 SCCR 216.
5 On sentencing, see the approach of the Court of Criminal Appeal in *Thomas v HM Advocate* (16 March 1990, 15 June 1990, unreported).

Mental handicap

10.09 A person who is severely mentally handicapped will be entitled to found on the plea of diminished responsibility. Sheriff Gordon states that there is no doubt that mental deficiency (as it was then called) usually does constitute diminished responsibility[1]. It is certainly clear now that the court in exercising its powers to make a hospital order under s 175 of the Criminal Procedure (Scotland) Act 1975 can do so when the mental disorder from which the accused suffered is a mental handicap[2]. It would accordingly be absurd and contrary to Parliament's intention as evidenced by the Mental Health (Scotland) Act 1984, for the courts to exclude mental handicap from the ambit of the plea of diminished responsibility.

1 *Gordon* para 11–24.
2 See the Mental Health (Scotland) Act 1984, s 17(1)(a)(ii).

11. Joint responsibility for crimes against the person

Art and part liability

11.01 The general rule of Scots law is that each person is only criminally liable for his own actions. However, there is one exception to this rule, apart from statutory considerations, and it was expressed by Lord Cameron thus:

'But if the Crown has proved beyond reasonable doubt that two or more persons have acted together in pursuance of a common criminal enterprise or purpose, then each of the persons proved to have been involved in that criminal enterprise or purpose is responsible for the acts of others in carrying out that common criminal enterprise'[1].

If, for example, A supplies B with a gun with which to shoot and kill C, A is liable for murder along with B. A's liability is on an 'art and part' basis. The expression 'art and part' is of ancient origin[2] but other phrases are commonly employed, such as 'acting in concert', 'aiding and abetting', and 'accession'. Art and part liability, however, only arises once it is proved affirmatively that there was a common plan and that the accused were parties to it[3].

1 *O'Connell v HM Advocate* 1987 SCCR 459 at 460. See also *Sinclair v HM Advocate* (4 May 1990, unreported), Court of Criminal Appeal.
2 See Mackenzie *The Laws and Customs of Scotland in Matters Criminal* (2nd edn, 1699) I, 35, 1; Hume *Commentaries* II, 225.
3 *HM Advocate v Lappen* 1956 SLT 109 at 110, per Lord Patrick.

Degrees of art and part liability

11.02 The degree of involvement of participants in a criminal enterprise can vary. Scots law, however, makes no distinction in the degrees of guilt between the actor (or principal) and the accomplice (or accessory)[1]. Both are equally guilty although at the sentencing stage the court can, where it is appropriate, reflect the differing degree of involvement in the criminal enterprise. The one exception to this is of course the case of murder where the sentence of life imprisonment is fixed by law, but it would be highly unlikely that a court would wish to make a distinction between the various participants who were each in law found to have committed a murderous assault. It is, however, possible for a jury to distinguish between the recklessness of the accused's actings in a case of homicide, and convict one accused of murder and another accused of only culpable homicide[2]. Such a discriminating verdict should normally only be justified if there are striking differences in the relevant conduct of each of the accused[3].

1 See J H A Macdonald *The Criminal Law of Scotland* (5th edn, 1948) p 2.
2 *Melvin v HM Advocate* 1984 SLT 365; and para 2.20, above.
3 *Malone v HM Advocate* 1988 SCCR 498; *Melvin v HM Advocate* 1984 SLT 365.

11.03 In terms of ss 46 and 312(d) of the Criminal Procedure (Scotland) Act 1975, when an accused person is charged on indictment or summary complaint it is not necessary to state that the accused is guilty actor or art and part. Such a charge is implied. It is, however, the general practice in certain circumstances for the Crown to libel specifically that the accused is charged with the offence in respect of his aiding and abetting it. The circumstances in which this will usually be done are when the accused is charged with an offence of which he could not be convicted as an actual perpetrator. Where a woman, for example, is charged with rape by barring the door and preventing the victim's escape, the Crown usually libels the specific acts which will amount to participation in the rape. Equally, before the decision in *Stallard v HM Advocate*[1] which removed a husband's immunity from prosecution for rape of his wife, the Crown would libel the specific acts which rendered him guilty as art and part in the rape. However, it has not at least in recent times, been a fatal objection to an indictment that such specification is omitted.

1 1989 SCCR 248.

Is the conviction of the principal essential to conviction of an accomplice?

11.04 In *Capuano v HM Advocate*[1] C was charged along with two other men with assaulting two people by throwing bricks and stones at their motor vehicle. One of the occupants was struck on the head by a stone. C's co-accused were acquitted but C was convicted. There was evidence that C had thrown or at least attempted to throw a missile at the motor vehicle; and that all three accused had participated in the attack. The Appeal Court held that the acquittal of the co-accused was not fatal to the conviction of C. The acquittal of C's co-accused did not mean that in the circumstances the jury were not entitled to convict C 'as a participant in the proved crime of assault committed by a group'. Of course, in *Capuano* all three accused were alleged actors but the Appeal Court recognised that there are cases in which if the only persons who could have committed an offence as actors have been acquitted, an accused cannot be found guilty art and part with them[2]. In *HM Advocate v Woods*[3] A's conviction for murder was quashed on the ground of misdirection on inter alia the trial judge's failure to direct the jury to acquit if they were in reasonable doubt as to A's guilt. A's two co-accused were convicted solely on the basis of acting in concert with A, and their convictions were also quashed. Guilt by accession presupposes that the crime has been established[4].

1 1984 SCCR 415.
2 *Young v HM Advocate* 1932 JC 63.
3 1972 SLT (Notes) 77.
4 *Macdonald* p 3.

Accession after the fact

11.05 Hume referred to an accused being guilty art and part of a crime on the basis inter alia of his 'approving of, or ratifying it after it is done'[1] but this is not the law in Scotland now, if indeed it ever was the law even when Hume wrote. Except in the case of treason, which is governed by English law, accession after the fact is not recognised in Scotland[2]. However, evidence of an accused's actings after for example, a murderous assault may go to prove a previously conceived plan to commit murder. Actings after the event can affect art and part guilt by demonstrating the existence of pre-existing concert.

1 *Hume* II, 225.
2 *Macdonald* p 8; *Gordon* paras 55, 57.

Dissociation

11.06 Sheriff Gordon states that in the case of a person who is allegedly art and part guilty of the crime by instigating its commission, an accused can avoid conviction by interrupting the chain of events leading from his instigation either by preventing the commission of the crime or at least by 'removing the influence of his instigation'[1]. In *Socratous v HM Advocate*[2] the Appeal Court rejected the concept of a defence of dissociation. The true question was to be seen in the context of possible concert. If a crime is merely in contemplation and preparations for it are being made, a participator who then quits the enterprise cannot be held to have acted in concert with those who go on to commit the crime because there will be no evidence that he played any part in its commission. Lord Justice-General Emslie further stated: 'If on the other hand the perpetration of a planned crime or offence has begun, a participant cannot escape liability for the completed crime by withdrawing before it has been completed unless, perhaps, he also takes steps to prevent its completion'[3].

1 *Gordon* para 5–14.
2 1987 SLT 244.
3 1987 SLT 244 at 245. See also *Macdonald* pp 5, 6.

Mobbing and rioting

11.07 The separate crime of mobbing and rioting is an exception to the normal rules of art and part guilt. A mob is a combination of persons sharing a common criminal purpose which proceeds to carry out that purpose by violence or intimidation by sheer force of numbers. A mob is regarded as having a will and purpose of its own and

'all the members of the mob contribute by their presence to the achievement of the mob's purpose ... even where only a few directly engage in the commission of this specific unlawful act which it is the mob's common purpose to commit'[1].

Thus if A is present within a great mob of tumultuously assembled people and members of the mob not including A, assault and murder a number of people, A can be guilty of the individual assaults and the murder as well as the separate crime of mobbing if A's presence can be shown to have countenanced or contributed to the unlawful objectives of the mob. A can be held responsible for the individual crimes committed by members of the mob by reason of his presence in the mob although his mere presence would not be sufficient to render him liable on an art and part basis[2]. The exception in the case of mobbing and rioting is permitted because of the threat to public order presented by 'a large congregation of disorderly persons'[3].

1 *Hancock v HM Advocate* 1981 JC 74 at 86.
2 *Gordon* para 40–13.
3 Alison *Principles* p 518.

Breach of the peace

11.08 There is no exception to the ordinary rules of art and part guilt in the case of breach of the peace. A breach of the peace may include acts of violence such as assaults, but for A to be convicted of such a charge of breach of the peace on the basis of concert with B, C, and D, the normal rules must be applied to determine whether A aided and abetted B, C and/or D[1]. It is necessary to show that A was party to a common criminal plan to do what had been done[2].

1 See M G A Christie *Breach of the Peace* paras 2.45–2.46.
2 *Winnik v Allan* 1986 SCCR 35. See also *MacNeill v Robertson* 1982 SCCR 468.

Conspiracy

11.09 Scots law recognises the inchoate crime of conspiracy. Conspiracy is the agreement of two or more persons to render one another assistance in doing an act—whether as end or as means to an end—which would be criminal if done by a single individual[1]. It is not a conspiracy for persons to agree to commit an act which is not criminal unless the objective of that act is in itself criminal. The essence of the crime is the agreement of the conspirators. Thus it is criminal conspiracy for persons to agree to commit assault, or robbery or murder or any other offence against the person. Conspiracy is a crime at common law and there is no good reason in principle why conspiracy to commit a criminal contravention of a statute should not also be criminal. Where the objective of the conspiracy is achieved, the crime ceases to be a conspiracy and the conspirators then are art and part guilty of the completed offence.

1 *Macdonald* p 185. See also the charge to the jury in *Sayers v HM Advocate* 1981 SCCR 312.

Incitement

11.10 Incitement is a crime at common law. It is the encouraging, instigating or inducing of a person to commit a crime and as such it is in truth an attempt at conspiracy. If A successfully induces B to agree to commit assault and robbery, their plan becomes a conspiracy, but if B refuses to participate in the crime, A is nonetheless guilty of the crime of incitement to commit assault and robbery.

Knowledge

11.11 In cases founded on art and part responsibility, or in cases of conspiracy, the Crown must prove knowledge on the part of the participants or conspirators of the common criminal enterprise[1]. Such knowledge is, of course, a matter of inference from the proved circumstances but if the facts from which the knowledge of the common criminal objective cannot be proved, the jury must acquit the accused[2].

1 *Gordon* para 5–30; *Hume* I, 276.
2 Cf *Sayers v HM Advocate* 1981 SCCR 312.

11.12 Equally, therefore, where A and B commit a housebreaking and in the course of it they come upon the householder, and B pulls out a knife and stabs the householder to death, the jury will be entitled to convict A of murder if the Crown demonstrates that A knew that B had a knife. The inference from that fact of A knowing B had a knife is inevitably that B would use the knife[1]. Similarly, if two housebreakers went with pistols or knives, or anything which satisfied the jury that they were prepared, by violence, to overcome any resistance which was offered, regardless of human life, then though only one inflicted the fatal injury, both would be responsible for the homicide[2].

1 Cf *Walker and Raiker v HM Advocate* 1985 SCCR 150.
2 *HM Advocate v Welsh and McLachlan* (1897) 5 SLT 137.

11.13 In approaching the question whether the Crown is entitled to a conviction against A and B for acting in concert in the commission of, for example, murder, the jury should be directed to approach the issue in two stages. First, the jury should consider what can be proved against each accused individually. Secondly, the jury should thereafter consider whether or not from the facts individually proved against A and B, an inference can positively be drawn beyond reasonable doubt that their individual actings were part of a common plan[1]. There can however be spontaneous concert such as occurs in a street brawl during which the victim is killed. But whether the concert arises spontaneously or is premeditated, the jury must approach the issue in these two stages or otherwise there is a material risk that the jury will convict an accused person on the basis of the evidence relating to his co-accused.

1 See *O'Connell v HM Advocate* 1987 SCCR 459.

12. Miscellaneous general defences

Necessity and coercion

12.01 Necessity and coercion are two general defences which require particular attention because while these defences are founded on the same basic principles and are to that extent similar, they are so regarded in Scots law as separate pleas which are viewed in entirely different ways.

Necessity

12.02 The plea of necessity as a matter of theory is based on the law's allowing an accused person to commit a criminal offence when circumstances have compelled him to do so. The accused is accordingly excused from punishment. In England such a plea is referred to as 'duress of circumstances' in contra-distinction to duress arising out of threats made by human beings[1], which equate to coercion in Scots law[2]. Professor Williams explains the principle thus: 'the law has to be broken to achieve a greater good'[3].

1 See Smith and Hogan *Criminal Law* (6th edn, 1988) p 224.
2 See para 12.06, below.
3 Williams *Text Book of Criminal Law* (2nd edn) p 597.

12.03 Scots law does not at present recognise necessity as a complete defence resulting in acquittal[1]. There is little reported judicial discussion of necessity but such as there is indicates that the only consequence of a successful plea of necessity is mitigation of sentence. However, in one sheriff court case (*Tudhope v Grubb*[2]), an accused was acquitted of a contravention of s 6(1) of the Road Traffic Act 1972 when the accused drove his motor car in order to escape from attackers. The sheriff held that necessity had been made out on the basis that the accused had been the innocent victim of an assault and that the accused had disclosed all of the details of the incident to the police at the first opportunity after the accident[3].

1 See P W Ferguson 'Necessity and Duress in Scots Law' [1986] Crim LR 103.

2 1983 SCCR 350.
3 *Tudhope v Grubb* 1983 SCCR 350 at 352.

12.04 *Tudhope v Grubb* was referred to by the High Court in *MacLeod v MacDougall*[1]. In that case the accused was convicted of a contravention of s 6(1) of the Road Traffic Act 1972 when he also drove his motor car in order to avoid assailants who had attacked him and who he feared might still be in his vicinity. The accused, however, drove his car past a stationary police vehicle and did not report the earlier assault to the police. The High Court refused the accused's appeal against conviction on the ground that when he was driving under the influence of alcohol the necessity had by then passed. The court in so holding expressly remarked that it was not necessary to reach any concluded decision on the question of whether a defence of necessity is available to a charge of driving with excess alcohol in one's breath. The court did, however, quash the accused's disqualification on the basis that special reasons existed for not disqualifying although it is difficult to understand how, if the necessity had passed, it could be a special reason any more than it could be a complete defence. In either case the necessity had ceased to be operating. It is also to be noted, however, that in *MacLeod v MacDougall* the court did not state categorically that necessity cannot justify acquittal. In the later case of *McNab v Guild*[2], the High Court also reserved its opinion on whether necessity could be a defence to a charge of reckless driving. In that case, however, Lord Justice-Clerk Ross stated:

'We agree with the Advocate Depute that such a defence could only be made out if the findings showed that at the material time the appellant was in immediate danger of life or serious injury'[3].

The court refused the appeal because there was no imminent danger in circumstances where the accused drove his van after having been subjected to unspecified threats and while one assailant jumped on the bonnet of the van and another attempted to open the driver's door. It therefore appears from *McNab v Guild* that it may be possible to establish necessity but that it will only operate as a complete defence in cases where the threatened harm is serious and immediate, or imminent. Such a test is an exacting requirement and is unlikely to be satisfied in most cases.

1 1988 SCCR 519.
2 1989 SCCR 138.
3 See also *R v Conway* [1989] RTR 35 at 40 and 41, per Wolf J.

12.05 From the recent development of law in *MacLeod v MacDougall* and *McNab v Guild*, it is possible that necessity will become recognised as a complete defence justifying acquittal, and will be equated to the extent of coercion. The test employed for coercion is provided by Hume and is discussed in paragraph **12.06**, infra. In any event, even if necessity is not to be recognised as a complete defence, it is undoubtedly a mitigating circumstance[1]. Thus, while such a case has not yet come before the courts, if an accused were, for example, charged with culpable homicide by driving his car in a reckless manner in order to avoid a naturally occurring danger to him, he could be entitled to a restricted sentence even though his driving was a deliberately chosen act on his part.

1 See *Graham v Annan* 1980 SLT 28; *Connorton v Annan* 1981 SCCR 307; *McLeod v MacDougall* 1988 SCCR 519. See also Wheatley *Road Traffic Law in Scotland* para 3.9.

Coercion

12.06 The defence of coercion is well established in Scots law and justifies the acquittal of an accused. Coercion is defined, and the standards to be met in order to found upon it are described, by Hume:

'But generally, and with relation to the ordinary condition of a well-regulated society, where every man is under the shield of the law, and has a means of resorting to the protection, this is at least somewhat a difficult plea, and can hardly be serviceable in the case of a trial for any atrocious crime, unless it have the support of these qualifications: (1) and immediate danger of death or great bodily harm; (2) an inability to resist the violence; (3) a backward and an inferior part in the perpetration; and (4) a disclosure of the fact, as well as restitution of the profit on the first safe and convenient occasion. For if the pannel takes a very active part in the enterprise, or conceal the fact, and detain his share of the profit, when restored to a state of freedom, either of these replies will serve in a great measure to elide his defence'[1].

The four qualifications have been authoritatively interpreted and approved by the High Court in *Thomson v HM Advocate*[2].

1 *Hume* I, 52 (numerals added).
2 1983 SLT 682. See Norrie 'The Defence of Coercion in Scots Criminal Law' 1984 SLT (News) 13.

12.07 In *Thomson*, the accused was convicted of armed robbery and firearms offences. He pled coercion. The trial judge directed the jury that the danger which coerced the accused required to be immediate and not in the future. The accused appealed on the grounds of misdirection, but the High Court refused the appeal holding that Scots law required the danger to be immediate[1]. As Anderson said[2]:

'[t]he threats must have had reference to present, not to future injury'. The court in *Thomson* went on, however, to stress that Hume was not laying down absolute rules but only providing guidelines. The first two tests were considered by the High Court to be conditions which had to be satisfied in order for the defence of coercion 'to get off the ground'³ and the other two tests were intended to measure the accused's credibility and reliability on the issue of the defence.

1 See also *HM Advocate v McCallum* (19 May 1977, unreported).
2 A M Anderson *The Criminal Law of Scotland* (2nd edn, 1904) p 16.
3 1983 SLT at 686–687.

Is coercion a defence to murder?

12.08 Hume stated that the plea of coercion could hardly be serviceable in the case of a trial for any atrocious crime, and it therefore seems highly unlikely that the court would permit coercion as a defence to a charge of murder. In *HM Advocate v Peters*¹ the trial judge allowed coercion to be intimated as the defence in the case of murder, but the defence was not allowed to go to the jury because the evidence to support it was insufficient. It is, however, submitted here that there is no good reason to restrict the application of coercion. If the evidence discloses that an accused was subjected to threats of immediate danger of death or serious injury, and he was unable to resist these threats, then the defence should be available whether the charge is armed robbery or murder or culpable homicide. The policy of the law in England has, however, excluded duress as a defence to murder². When the opportunity arises the courts in Scotland will no doubt follow the English example.

1 (1969) 33 JCL 209.
2 *R v Howe* [1987] 1 All ER 771 overruling *Lynch v DPP for Northern Ireland* [1975] AC 653.

Insanity

12.09 Insanity is one of the four special defences of which notice requires to be given¹. The effect of a plea of insanity is acquittal. The accused is found not guilty by reason of his insanity at the time of the commission of the crime². The defence is, of course, a general defence and can be advanced in answer to any criminal charge with the exception, perhaps, of a defence which does not require the proof of any form of *mens rea* at all, where liability is absolute. The practical use of the insanity defence in present times is, however, severely restricted since the principal advantage of the defence was removed by the abolition of the death penalty in 1965. On an accused being acquitted on the ground of insanity the court must make an order for the detention of the accused in a State hospital or if there are special reasons, in some other specified hospital. The accused's detention is without limit of time[3].

1 J H A Macdonald *The Criminal Law of Scotland* (5th edn, 1948) p 265.
2 Criminal Procedure (Scotland) Act 1975, s 174(2).
3 Ibid, s 174(3).

The definition of insanity

12.10 In *HM Advocate v Kidd*[1] Lord Strachan, when directing the jury, posed the question: 'What nature and degree of mental illness is sufficient in law to excuse a person from responsibility for his actions?'. Lord Strachan answered the question in the following terms:

'The question really is, whether at the time of the offence of which he is charged the accused was of unsound mind... Treat it broadly, and treat the question as being whether the accused was of sound or unsound mind. The question is primarily one of fact to be decided by you... First, in order to excuse a person from responsibility for his acts on the ground of insanity, there must have been an alienation of the reason in relation to the act committed. There must have been some mental defect, to use a broad neutral word, a mental defect, by which his reason was overpowered and he was thereby rendered incapable of exerting his reason to control his conduct and reactions. If his reason was alienated in relation to the act committed, he was not responsible for that act, even although otherwise he may have been apparently quite rational. What is required is some alienation of the reason in relation to the act committed'.

Thereafter Lord Strachan directed the jury that the question was to be answered in the light of the evidence by the jury using their common-sense and knowledge of mankind, and while they had to have regard to medical opinion, the medical evidence by itself was not to be regarded by them as conclusive[2].

1 1960 JC 61.
2 See also *HM Advocate v Blake* 1986 SLT 661.

12.11 It is clear from Lord Strachan's directions in *Kidd* that insanity in Scots law is constituted by an alienation of reason in relation to the act committed. The accused's reason must be overpowered by mental defect which makes him incapable of exerting his reason to control his conduct in the particular circumstances of the case. This approach is the one which was stated by Hume in the eighteenth century. Hume defined insanity as an absolute alienation of reason,

'such a disease as deprives a patient of the knowledge of the true aspect and position of things about him... and gives him up to the impulse of his own distempered fancy'[1].

Hume's definition, moreover, has been approved by a court of seven judges in *Brennan v HM Advocate*[2] where the court stated that they had no doubt that the law as stated by Hume is and always has been the law of Scotland. This observation is regrettable since it ignores the fact that at least for a certain period in the history of Scots law, the McNaghten Rules[3] were incorporated into Scots law[4].

1 *Hume* I, 37.
2 1977 SLT 151.
3 *McNaghten's Case* (1843) 10 Cl & Fin 200.
4 See *Gordon* paras 10–25 to 10–27.

The McNaghten Rules

12.12 The McNaghten Rules were concerned primarily with determining whether an accused person was insane by a consideration of the accused's knowledge of the nature and quality of the criminal act, or at least his knowledge that he was doing something that was wrong. It is quite clear, however, that a man can know what he is doing and know that it is both immoral and criminal, and yet still be insane. For example, pyromaniacs who deliberately set fire to property to be thrilled by the sight of destruction, are usually perfectly aware of what they are doing and that what they are doing is criminal. They may nonetheless be clinically insane and capable of psychiatric treatment. It is therefore inappropriate to hold that they are not legally insane. The definition of legal insanity provided by Hume acknowledges this difficulty and so directs inquiry to the general mental condition of the accused, or as Hume expressed it, 'the whole circumstances of the situation'. A man may know that murder is wrong but his insane delusion may make him believe that he is acting in self-defence or fighting and evil spirit[1], and he should still be acquitted by reason of his insanity.

1 *Macdonald* p 9.

12.13 Insanity can be temporary. An accused can be insane at the time of the event and recover thereafter, but he is still entitled to be acquitted of the crime. The important consideration is whether the accused has suffered an absolute alienation of reason[1]. Thus, an accused who suffers only from oddness or eccentricity, however strong his oddness or eccentricity may be, is not legally insane. However, an accused may also be insane because of his own conduct. A distinction can be drawn between a man who is so chronically alcoholic that his brain has deteriorated through the effects of alcohol such that he is mentally deranged, and a man of whom it can only be said that he is incapable of forming the necessary criminal intent because of his consumption of alcohol[2]. In the latter case the Court in *Brennan v HM Advocate*[3] held that there could not be insanity or diminished responsibility. However, *Brennan* only dealt with transient self-induced intoxication and not with long established mental impairment through chronic alcoholism. It is therefore undecided whether insanity is available to an accused in the former case although it is here submitted that consideration of public policy may well require that such a person who is no doubt incapable of medical cure, should be dealt with as a criminal.

1 *Brennan v HM Advocate* 1977 SLT 151; *HM Advocate v Kidd* 1960 JC 61.
2 *Macdonald* p 10.
3 1977 SLT 151.

Onus of proof

12.14 The onus of proof in the case of insanity, unlike any other of the special defences, rests on the accused[1]. This burden flows from the existence of a rebuttable presumption of sanity. Since the courts proceed on the assumption that all men are sane until the contrary is proved, it is for the accused to prove that at the time of the offence he was insane. The standard of proof, however, is the lower civil requirement of proof on balance of probability.

1 *Lambie v HM Advocate* 1973 SLT 219.

Intoxication

12.15 In *Brennan v HM Advocate*[1] the accused who was charged with murdering his father by stabbing him, had drunk between 20 and 25 pints of beer and a glass of sherry and had consumed a microdot of LSD shortly before the fatal act. It was argued on appeal that the trial judge had erred in refusing to direct the jury that if intoxication were established they could reduce the crime from murder to culpable homicide. The appeal court rejected that contention on the basis of public policy. The Court, overruling *HM Advocate v Campbell*[2] and *Kennedy v HM Advocate*[3], held that there was nothing unethical or unfair or contrary to the general principles of Scots law that self-induced intoxication is not by itself a defence to any criminal charge. Self-induced intoxication taken together with the accused's other actings added up, in the opinion of the court, to criminal recklessness sufficient for murder.

1 1977 SLT 151.
2 1921 JC 1.
3 1944 JC 171.

Involuntary intoxication

12.16 Since the underlying rationale of *Brennan* was that people who deliberately drink to excess should not be allowed to found upon that self-induced intoxication in order to secure acquittal or a reduction of the charge to culpable homicide, it could be argued that involuntary intoxication should be a valid defence because the accused in these circumstances is not guilty of creating his own incapacity. Such a view is, however, not accepted in Scotland. In *McGregor v HM Advocate*[1] the Appeal Court was invited to assent to the proposition that

'if a jury accepts that a drug was administered to the accused without his knowledge, and if they accept also that he had no criminal intent and the reason for that was the administration of the drug, they are bound to acquit'.

The Court refused to endorse that proposition and while *McGregor* is not an authority on uninduced intoxication, it cannot be doubted that if the question ever comes before the Appeal Court the court will reject the concept of involuntary intoxication (whether by drink or drugs) as a defence to a criminal charge. Lord McCluskey has, however, contradicted this view in his charge to the jury in *HM Advocate v Raiker*[2] but the preferable view is contained in *McGregor*.

1 (1973) SCCR Supp 54.
2 1989 SCCR 149 at 154.

Automatism and involuntary conduct

12.17 Scots law does not recognise a defence which has come to be known in England and the Commonwealth countries as automatism. Automatism is involuntary conduct on the part of an accused. A driver of a motor car may, for example, be suddenly stung by a bee and collide with an oncoming car. The collision is involuntary and that fact could therefore be a ground for acquittal if the law recognised such a defence. The most common forms of automatic conduct are somnambulism and epileptic fits.

12.18 Until the decision in *HM Advocate v Cunningham*[1] there had been a few reported cases in which automatism was recognised as a valid defence. In *Simon Fraser*[2] the accused was charged with murdering his baby son by fracturing his skull. The accused had been asleep and while asleep had killed his son in the unconscious belief that he (the accused) was being attacked by an animal. The jury were directed to ignore any question of insanity and were invited to return a verdict that the accused had killed his son but that he was unconscious by reason of somnambulism, and that he was therefore not responsible. In *HM Advocate v Hayes*[3] the accused was charged with culpable homicide or alternatively reckless driving. He had driven a bus which collided with two stationary vehicles, and thereby killed some of the passengers. The jury found the accused guilty of culpable homicide but also found a 'special defence' established that the accused had been suffering from temporary dissociation at the time by reason of masked epilepsy or other pathological condition. Lord Carmont certified the case to the High Court. A Full Bench advised Lord Carmont that if the accused were to give an undertaking never to drive any motor vehicle again he should be discharged from the Bar[4].

1 1963 JC 80, 1963 SLT 345.
2 (1878) 4 Coup 70.
3 (November 1949, unreported), High Court of Justiciary.
4 See also *HM Advocate v Ritchie* 1926 JC 45.

12.19 The law is now, however, stated in *HM Advocate v Cunningham*[1] which must be taken to overrule the earlier cases insofar as they suggest that Scots law recognises the validity of a defence of automatism. The accused in *Cunningham* was charged with inter alia causing death by reckless driving. He lodged a 'special defence' that he was not responsible for his actings on account of the incidence of temporary dissociation due to an epileptic fugue or other pathological condition. The trial judge certified the case to the High Court at Edinburgh which advised that it was not a defence which could result in acquittal. For acquittal the accused would require to demonstrate insanity (which would no doubt have been possible but would have resulted in the accused being detained under the Mental Health (Scotland) Act 1960). Lord Justice-General Clyde in giving the advice of the court, said:

'Any mental or pathological condition short of insanity—any question of diminished responsibility owing to any cause, which does not involve insanity—is relevant only to the question of mitigating circumstances and sentence'.

This statement of the law, although in some cases it has been ignored[2], has been recently approved in *Carmichael v Boyle*[3] where Lord Justice-Clerk Wheatley made clear that the authority of the decision in *Cunningham* could only be superseded by an Act of Parliament or by a larger constituted court.

1 1963 JC 80, 1963 SLT 345.
2 See eg *Farrell v Stevenson* 1975 SLT (Sh Ct) 71 and *Stirling v Annan* 1983 SCCR 396.
3 1985 SCCR 58, 1985 SLT 399.

12.20 In *Carmichael v Boyle* the accused was acquitted by the sheriff of charges of assault and breach of the peace on the ground that the accused was in a state of hypoglycaemia when he committed the act and that the evil intent necessary for the crimes had accordingly not been proved. The High Court rejected the sheriff's approach and held that if the acts were proved then an inference of *mens rea* was inevitable unless the accused proved that he was insane as defined in *HM Advocate v Kidd*[1] and *Brennan v HM Advocate*[2]. Accordingly, if an accused wishes to be acquitted on the ground of mental incapacity, he must plead insanity. If he cannot or will not plead insanity, his mental incapacity can only at best result in mitigation of his sentence.

1 1960 JC 61.
2 1977 SLT 151.

Index

Accident
self defence and, 8.17, 8.18
Accomplice
conviction of principal, and, 11.04
Adultery
provocation, as, 9.06
Aggravated assault
breach of trust, 1.13
generally, 1.04–1.15
Macdonald's definition, 1.06
objective determination of, 1.04
place of crime, 1.08–1.09
trial of, 1.05
use of weapon, 1.07
victim, character of, 1.10, 1.12
   knowledge of, 1.14
Aiding and abetting. *See* ART AND PART
Art and part
accession after the fact, 11.05
breach of the peace, 11.08
co-accused, conviction of, 11.04
conspiracy, 11.09
degrees of guilt, 11.02
dissociation from crime, 11.06
example, 11.01
exception to rule, 11.07
knowledge of participants, 11.11–11.13
meaning, 11.01
rape, and, 11.03
sentencing differentials, 11.02
specific libel of charge of, 11.03
Assault
aggravated. *See* AGGRAVATED ASSAULT
attempted, 1.02
breach of trust, 1.13
culpable homicide. *See* CULPABLE HOMICIDE
culpable and reckless conduct. *See* CULPABLE AND RECKLESS CONDUCT
danger of life, to, trial of, 1.05
death as result of, 3.05

Assault—*continued*
defences to—
   children, discipline of, 1.27–1.28
   consent, 1.16–1.19
   lawful use of force. 1.20–1.29
   prevention of crime, 1.23–1.26
   self defence, 1.21–1.22
doctrine of transferred intent, 1.03
examples, 1.01, 1.03
intent to commit further crime, 1.15
meaning, 1.01
mens rea, 1.03, 1.17–1.18
officers of law, on, 1.12
precincts of court, within, 1.09
private defence, 1.21–1.22
property, in defence of, 1.29
robbery distinguished, 5.03–5.05
Sovereign, on, 1.11
Attempted murder
provocation and, 9.12
Automatism, 12.17–12.20
examples in Scots law, 12.18
insanity and, 12.18–12.20
statement of current law, 12.19, 12.20

Breach of the peace, 11.08
Breach of trust
assault, and, 1.13
incest, and, 6.07

Child
discipline of, 1.20, 1.27–1.28
sexual intercourse with, 6.07
   defences to, 6.07
Child *in utero*
injury to, 2.01
Citizen's arrest, 1.25–1.26
Coercion
meaning, 12.06
murder, defence to, 12.08
qualifications to, 12.06, 12.07

Consent
defence, as
  assault, 1.16–1.19
  rape, 1.19, 4.04–4.06
Conspiracy, 11.09
knowledge of criminal purpose, 11.11
Criminal homicide. *See* HOMICIDE
Culpable homicide, 3.01 *et seq*
assault, and, 3.04, 3.05
categories of, 3.01
distinguished from murder, 3.07
examples of, 3.06
involuntary, 3.01, 3.03
  negligence, by, 3.08–3.12
  recklessness, by, 3.08–3.12
penalties, 3.05, 3.06
recklessness, 3.09–3.12
voluntary, 3.01, 3.02
Culpable and reckless conduct
assault and, 1.30–1.33
common law and statutory standards, 1.31
death as result of, 3.05, 3.06
examples of criminal, 1.32
Roberts v Hamilton, 1.30
test for, 1.31, 1.33

Death
meaning, 2.02
Death sentence
justifiable homicide, as, 2.05
Defences
accident, 8.17
automatism, 12.17–12.20
coercion, 12.01, 12.06–12.08
consent, 1.16–1.19
diminished responsibility, 10.01 *et seq*
insanity, 12.09–12.14
intoxication, 12.15, 12.16
necessity, 12.01, 12.02–12.05
novus actus interveniens, 2.11
provocation, 8.05, 8.06, 9.01 *et seq*
  rape, to, 4.04–4.06
self defence, 1.21–1.22, 8.01 *et seq*
Diminished responsibility, 10.01 *et seq*
crimes other than murder, 10.07
meaning, 10.02
mental handicap, 10.09
onus of proof, 10.06
psychopathic personality, 10.03–10.05
restrictions on defence of, 10.03, 10.04
sentencing, effect on, 10.07, 10.08
Doctrine of transferred intent
assault, 1.03

Extortion, 5.06

Hamesucken, 1.08
Hijacking
generally, 5.13
Tokyo Convention Act 1967 . . . 5.13
Homicide
attempted, 3.13
casual, 2.04
classes of, 2.03
committed in course of another crime, 2.19–2.20, 3.04–3.07
criminal—
  death from emotional shock, 2.08–2.09
  generally, 2.06–2.09
  omission, caused by, 2.06
  reckless driving, 3.10–3.11
culpable. *See* CULPABLE HOMICIDE
defence, accident, 8.17
joint responsibility, 11.12
justifiable, 2.05
  death sentence, 2.05
  killing by armed forces, 2.05
  necessity, 2.05
  sentence by magistrate, 2.05
meaning, 2.01
mistaken belief of attack, 8.15, 8.16
property, defence of, 8.14
robbery, in course of, 2.20
self defence, 8.01
'thin skull' rule, 2.10
Homosexual act
limited decriminalisation, 7.03
procuring or attempting to procure, 7.04

Incest
meaning, 6.01
prohibited degrees of relationship, 6.01–6.03
statutory defences to, 6.04
Incitement, 11.10
Insanity, 12.09–12.14
alcohol consumption, and, 12.13
automatism, and, 12.19, 12.20
considerations for jury, 12.10
effect of plea of, 12.09
Hume's definition, 12.11
meaning, 12.10–12.11
McNaghten Rules, 12.12
onus of proof, 12.14
temporary, 12.13

Intention
commit further crime, to, 1.15
Intoxication, 12.13
involuntary, 12.16
self-induced, 12.15
Involuntary conduct. *See* AUTOMATISM
Involuntary culpable homicide. *See* CULPABLE HOMICIDE

Joint responsibility
considerations for jury, 11.13
And see ART AND PART

Knowledge
art and part liability, 11.11–11.13
conspiracy, participants in, 11.11

Lewd, indecent and libidinous practices, 7.05–7.08
examples of, 7.05
extension of offence, 7.06

Malregimen, 2.13
Marriage
rape in, 4.01
McNaghten Rules, 12.12
Mens rea
assault, 1.03, 1.17–1.18
determination of, 2.18
murder, 2.14–2.18
reckless driving, 3.12
robbery, 5.02
theft, 5.02
Mental handicap
diminished responsibility, 10.09
Mob
meaning, 11.07
Mobbing and rioting, 11.07
Murder
attempted, 2.15
culpable homicide distinguished, 3.07
defence—
 coercion, 12.08
 diminished responsibility, 10.01
 provocation, 9.01
meaning, 2.14
mens rea, 2.14–2.18
 determination of, 2.18
 intent to do serious bodily harm, 2.16
 wicked recklessness, and, 2.14–2.17

Necessity
English law, 12.02
justifiable homicide, and, 2.05
reckless driving, 12.03–12.04

Necessity—*continued*
Scots law, 12.03–12.05
successful plea, result, 12.03–12.05
test for, 12.04
Novus actus interveniens
defence to homicide, 2.11
malregimen, as, 2.13
test for, 2.11, 2.13

Officers of law
assault on, 1.12
Onus of proof
diminished responsibility, 10.06
insanity, 12.14
self defence, 8.03

Piracy
generally, 5.08–5.10
Tokyo Convention Act 1967, 5.11–5.12
Prevention of crime
police officer, by, 1.23
private person, by, 1.24–1.26
reasonable use of force, 1.23–1.26
Property
defence of—
 assault, 1.29
 homicide, 8.14
Provocation
adultery, and, 9.06
attempted murder, and, 9.12
cumulative, 9.08
defence as, generally, 9.01
delay, effect of, 9.07
indirect, 9.10
murder, defence to, 8.05, 8.06
reasonable error, 9.11
reasonableness of retaliation, 9.09
requirements of, 9.03
 reasonable use of force, 9.05
 serious assault, 9.04, 9.05
self defence and, 8.04, 8.05, 9.02
Psychopathic personality, 10.03–10.05
Puberty
age of in law, 7.05

Rape
absence of force, 4.08
art and part liability, 11.03
attempted, 4.06
consent, and, 1.19, 4.04–4.06
defence to killing rapist, 8.12
drugging of victim, 4.10
establishment of, 4.02
girl legally incapable of consent, 4.11
husband, by, 4.01

Rape—*continued*
meaning, 4.01, 4.03
prostitute of, 4.01
use of force, 4.07
Reasonable use of force
children, discipline of, 1.20, 1.27–1.28
prevention of crime, 1.20–1.26
Recklessness
culpable homicide, and, 3.09–3.11
meaning for common law crimes, 3.10
murder, and, 2.14–2.17
rape, and, 4.06
road traffic legislation, 3.10–3.12
Robbery
assault distinguished, 5.03–5.05
homicide in course of, 2.20
meaning, 5.01
mens rea, 5.02
proof of violence, 5.03–5.05
theft distinguished, 5.01
threats and intimidation, 5.06–5.07

Self defence
accident and, 8.17, 8.18
assault and, 1.21–1.22
burden of proof, 8.03
considerations for jury, 8.06
effect of, 8.03
excessive use of force, 8.05
homicide, 8.01
justifiable homicide, as, 2.05
mens rea of accused, 8.03
objective justification for, 8.15, 8.16
private defence, as, 8.02
provocation distinguished, 8.04, 8.05
provocation, and, 9.02
rape, extension of defence to, 8.12
requirements of, 8.07–8.11
  danger to life, 8.08
  imminent danger, 8.09
  no means of escape, 8.10
  reasonable use of force, 8.11
sodomy, not available as defence, 8.13

Sentencing
art and part liability, effect of, 11.02
diminished responsibility, effect of, 10.07, 10.08
Sexual intercourse
meaning, 6.08
mentally deficient or mentally ill woman, 4.12
mistaken identity, 4.09
sleeping woman, with, 4.08
step-child, with, 6.05
statutory defence, 6.06
Shamelessly indecent conduct, 6.09
Sodomy
limited decriminalisation of, 7.03
homicide to prevent, 8.13
meaning, 7.02
woman with, 7.02
Step-child
sexual intercourse with, 6.05
defences to, 6.06
Suicide, 2.01
mortally injured victim, by, 2.12
novus actus interveniens, and, 2.12

Theft
mens rea, 5.02
Threats
robbery, and, 5.06–5.07
Tokyo Convention Act 1967, 5.11–5.13
Treason, 1.11, 11.05
Trial
assault to the danger of life, of, 1.05

Unlawful sexual intercourse, 7.07, 7.08
'clandestine injury to women', 4.13
defence to charge, 7.08

Voluntary culpable homicide, 3.02